From Tavern to Temple
ST. PETER'S CHURCH, AUBURN:
THE FIRST CENTURY

From Tavern to Temple
St. Peter's Church, Auburn:
The First Century

Robert Curtis Ayers, Ph.D.

Cloudbank Creations, Inc.
Scottsdale, Arizona
2005

From Tavern to Temple
St. Peter's Church, Auburn:
The First Century

Copyright © 2005
by Robert Curtis Ayers

Cover design by Trisha Hadley

Book design by Steven E. Swerdfeger, Ph.D.,
a former organist and Warden of the Parish

All rights reserved. No part of this book may be used or reproduced in any manner whatsoever without written permission except in the case of brief quotations embodied in articles and reviews.

Published by

Cloudbank Creations, Inc.
6137 East Mescal Street
Scottsdale, Arizona 85254-5418

www.CloudbankCreations.com

ISBN: 1-932842-13-6 (Cloth) — $ 39.95
ISBN: 1-932842-14-4 (Paper) — $ 24.95

Library of Congress Control Number: 2005928039

Printed in the United States of America

In memory of

JOHN HATCH CHEDELL AND JOHN BRAINARD

"And they gave the money, being told,
into the hands of them that did the work...
and they laid it out to the carpenters and builders,
that wrought upon the house of the Lord."
—Second Kings 12:11

Contents

	Page
PREFACE	i
CHAPTER 1 From Bostwick's Tavern to Dr. Rudd's Stone Church	1
Excursus I: John Rudd Calls for a Parsonage	31
Excursus II: Hobart Churchmanship versus the Second Great Awakening	35
CHAPTER 2 Death, Delay, and 'Departure for Higher Service' Ministries of William Lucas, Charles Hackley, and William Croswell, 1833 — 1844	45
Excursus III: Arthur Cleveland Coxe Visits St. Peter's Church, 1835	59
CHAPTER 3 Samuel Hanson Coxe, Jr., Comes and Goes, 1844 — 1846	65
CHAPTER 4 Pastoral Progress. The Ministry of Walter Ayrault, 1847 — 1852	73
Excursus IV: People of Color	87

CHAPTER 5 — 91
Ministries of E. H. Cressey, C. H. Platt, and
J.W. Pierson, 1852 — 1863: The Civil War Begins

CHAPTER 6 — 101
The Sewards and Religion

CHAPTER 7 — 127
The Magnificent Patron, John Hatch Chedell

Excursus V: The Oswego Starch Company — 139

CHAPTER 8 — 147
Women and St. Peter's

CHAPTER 9 — 159
The Brainard Era, 1863 — 1906
War Leads on to the Gilded Age

CHAPTER 10 — 193
How John Brainard Became Auburn

APPENDIX A — 207
The Death of Bishop Hobart

APPENDIX B — 213
The Rejected Successor's Sensational End

Preface

It was my pleasure to serve as the Rector of the Episcopal Church of Saints Peter and John in Auburn, New York from 1988 to 1998. Several years before that the ancient parish of St. Peter's had merged with St. John's, Auburn, joining two churches which had been separate since 1868.

The grand old flagship parish of St. Peter's had an illustrious past, but had fallen on difficult times, and a merger gradually resulted in new life for it and for the Episcopalian way of worship in Auburn. During the years in which I was privileged to oversee the reestablishment of the parish as a viable entity, as well as the protracted and expensive repairs which brought the church and the adjacent parish house back into stable condition, I developed a profound awareness of the heritage which St. Peter's represents.

One element of good fortune in that heritage is that many of the vital documents relating to St. Peter's history have survived. The parish registers are complete from the beginning around 1803 until the present. The Vestry Minutes which cover the parish business from the very first days of the organization on through the opening decade of the twentieth century are intact in one volume. The daily journals of the official acts of two important ministers, Walter Ayrault and John Brainard, have been preserved. Dr. Brainard's journals of his long ministry fill three large volumes. He saved countless items of ephemera and correspondence and had them bound into memory books which illuminate much of his interests and activity. [I regret that a similar record book of John Rudd's was reportedly discovered in Utica almost a decade ago, but has disappeared.]

Frances Miller Seward, the wife of William Henry Seward, wrote to him, usually from Auburn, almost every day, and she often mentioned events at St. Peter's in her diary-like letters. The prominence of the Sewards caused these letters to be preserved and I was able to examine them extensively with trips to the Rush Rhees Library of the University of Rochester. While doing so I gained a sincere appreciation for Auburn's own Earl Conrad, author of the 1960 work of interpretative history, *The Governor and His Lady*. Earl Conrad's sensitive understanding of the relationship between Mrs. Seward and her frequently absent husband is firmly supported by an examination of her letters.

Sometime in the past an *omnium gatherum* of materials from the once prominent Auburn law firm of William Allen, Alonzo G. Beardsley, and Theodore Pomeroy, was acquired by the Rare Book, Manuscript and Special Collections Library of Duke University, where they are catalogued as the "Alonzo Beardsley Papers." Several years ago I was able to spend a week in Durham extracting from them some very helpful knowledge about, among other things, the Oswego Starch Company.

In the course of writing this book I have been assisted by a number of persons. The late Malcolm Goodelle, once Archivist of Cayuga County, always knew where to find anything in his collections. Mrs. Mary Gilmore, who presides over the History Room at Auburn's Seymour Library, has willingly shared her knowledge and resources, and I thank her deeply. Her enthusiasm for Auburn's intriguing past encourages every inquiry.

At the University of Rochester I received a hearty welcome and great cooperation from Nancy Martin, Director of the Rare Book and Special Collections division of the Rush Rhees Library. Janie C. Morris, Research Services Librarian of the Duke University Rare Book,

Manuscripts and Special Collections Library, not only sent me a detailed index of the Alonzo Beardsley Papers but was of real assistance during my visit.

The current Rector of the Church of Saints Peter and John, the Rev. Douglas Taylor-Weiss, suggested to me that I should write a full history of the church in time for the bicentennial celebration in 2005. I reluctantly agreed to perform the task, and so the book has emerged with his support, for which I am grateful, but, partly because of the nature of the surviving materials, I have dealt only with the first century.

Very special thanks are reserved for Cynthia McFarland, known to countless thousands as the co-editor of Anglicans Online [anglicansonline.org]. From the outset of my project I have been able to consult with her, and she has graciously contributed two selections to this work from her own wide-ranging researches.

Like many current writers I am indebted to all the resources which have been placed on the Internet. Fact checking is so much facilitated by the work of those who have made so much available. And I am particularly thankful for the posting of the old City Directories of Auburn, and for the listing of the interments in Fort Hill cemetery. I have compiled a new complete account of the interments in St. Peter's Churchyard and I hope to see that list posted in the future.

The year 2005 marks the Bicentennial of St. Peter's Episcopal Church. It is Auburn's oldest incorporated body, predated only by the County Court. I hope that those who read my attempt to sketch out this portion of the past will be encouraged to preserve Auburn's heritage.

ROBERT CURTIS AYERS

395

therein follow it to be Recorded

Sebastian Visscher
Master in Ch.y

At a meeting of a number of the Inhabitants of the town of Aurelius in the County of Cayuga members of the Protestant Episcopal Church in the State of New York duly notified and held at the dwelling house of Doctr. Hezekiah Burt in the said town of Aurelius on the first Day of July A.D. one thousand eight hundred and five for the purpose of electing Wardens and Vestrymen of the Church to be there organized Agreable to an act of the Legislature Entitled an Act to provide for the incorperation of religious Societies pass-ed the twenty seventh day of March one thousand eight hundred and one. Present the Revd. Davenport Phelps Missionary of the Protestant Episcopal Church in the State of New York in the Chair. Thomas Jefferies Esqr. Jonathan Higby, Timothy Hatch, Ebenezer Phelps, John Pierson, William Bostwick and Joel Lake. After reading prayers proceded to the Choice of Wardens and Vestrymen. When William I. Vredenburgh Esqr. and Doctor Hezekiah Burt were unanimously elected Wardens. and Messrs. Thomas Jefferies Esqr. Jonathan Booth, Timothy Hatch, William Bostwick, Jeduthan Higby, Joel Lake, John Pierson, and Ebenezer Phelps were unanimously chosen Vestry-men. Moved and Seconded that Monday in Easter week both the day fixed on for the annual election of their Successors and that the said Church in Aurelius shall forever hereafter be known by the name or title of Saint Peters Church both which were unanimously resolved in the Affirmative.

Davenport Phelps Missionary of the Protestant Episcopal Church in the State of New York

Jeduthun Higby .... LS
Thomas Jefferies .... LS
William Bostwick .... LS

Cayuga County ss: On the 7th day May 1806 before me Joseph Annin one of the Judges of the Court of Common Pleas for said County. Came Jonathan Higby, Thomas Jefferies and William Bostwick severally Acknowledged that they executed the forgoing Instrument as their Voluntary act & Deed Therefore let the same be Recorded

Jos Annin

A copy of the original 1805 Charter for St. Peter's Church

THE FIRST S. PETER'S CHURCH, AUBURN
1812

Chapter 1

FROM BOSTWICK'S TAVERN TO DR. RUDD'S STONE CHURCH

The beginnings of St. Peter's Church in Auburn have often been told. The earliest written version we have is the *Historical Sketch* authored by the Rev. Dr. John C. Rudd in 1833. He began by recounting William Bostwick's origins in Connecticut, which he termed "that prolific hive of valuable population."

The development of the Episcopal Church in Auburn was heavily indebted to the migration westward along the "Great Road" which began in Connecticut and ran from Albany to the Genesee country. In 1788, canal planner Elkanah Watson was impressed by the large numbers of settlers moving up the valley of the Mohawk from "the Connecticut hive, with its annual swarms of industrious and enterprising immigrants, so highly qualified to overcome and civilize the wilderness."[1] It was said that on one winter's day in Albany in 1795 five hundred sleighs passed westward. In summer twenty boats a day went up the Mohawk River.[2] Many of these migrants were adherents of the Protestant Episcopal Church in Connecticut, where membership in that church was taken very seriously. Connecticut, with its neighbor, Long Island, possessed strong churchmen, and in 1783 the former region had produced the American denomination's first bishop, Samuel Seabury.

---

[1] Peter L. Bernstein, *Wedding of the Waters* (New York: Norton, 2005), 87.
[2] Stewart W. Holbrook, *The Yankee Exodus* (New York, 1950), 37.

From Tavern

At the end of the colonial period Connecticut's population was expanding almost geometrically due to the increase in birthrate.[3] This rapid growth in young people contributed to the new population of the military tract of Aurelius and provided a number of strong Episcopalians. Their devotion to Church and Prayer Book eventually led to separation from their Congregational-Presbyterian neighbors, brought about when William Bostwick, a devout Episcopalian and well versed in churchly ways, ventured one Sunday, in the absence of a protestant minister, to conduct Morning Prayer for the union worship held in his tavern.

Here is Rudd's account:

> The first settlement of this village, then embraced in the Military Township of Aurelius, was made by John Hardenbergh, in the year 1793, or 1794. Not long after him WILLIAM BOSTWICK, a most liberal and enterprising man from Connecticut, that prolific hive of valuable population for the then 'very far west,' made his lodgment on the west side of the outlet of the Owasco Lake, and as the writer has been informed, felled the first tree, laid low by a settler, with his own hands, on the lot that is now occupied by a very large proportion of the village. This man, with a few others who followed him, held a devoted attachment to the Protestant Episcopal Church. Such however was the paucity of numbers around him, really attached to this communion; and such was the prejudice that prevailed towards it, as a 'sect everywhere spoken

---

[3] George L. Clark, *A History of Connecticut: Its People and Institutions* (New York, 1914), 35.

against' that for a long time, the idea of organizing an Episcopal Congregation did not enter their minds. The few Churchmen in the vicinity being men of excellent character and habits, held their rank in society and were accredited as valuable citizens. They attended the only religious services found there, and conducted as religious men, in the desire to promote the prosperity of sound piety and good morals. These services were for years attended in the *Large Room* of Mr. Bostwick's House, which was devoted to the accommodation of Travellers. This room was by turns a Court House – a Church – a Ball Room, and a convenience for various uses, to which an infant settlement might wish to appropriate it. Mr. Bostwick, on the organization of a Presbyterian, or Congregational Society was made a Trustee, and in that capacity served the society with great fidelity and advantage, always however declaring his attachment to the Episcopal Church and services, and always enjoying the respect and affection of those, who though different in faith from himself, regarded him as an excellent man.

In process of time it happened that in the absence of the minister who then was, it is believed the only teacher here in spiritual things, Mr. Bostwick aided by another, read the services of the Episcopal Church and sermon, in the usual place of meeting. This was done by a general wish of the people; but on the return of the minister a great change was soon produced. The sermon on the subsequent Sunday was a severe rebuke to the worthy men who had dared before the population of the then small village to read the Liturgy of the Protestant Episcopal Church. This undeserved assault upon the usages and principles of his communion and his well meant attention to the duty of public worship, at once created a division from the then established order of things, and resulted in the organization of an Episcopal congregation under the name of ST. PETER'S CHURCH.[4]

St. Peter's congregation came into informal existence in 1803, when visiting clergy began to make entries of pastoral acts in the first parish register, a small book maintained by William Bostwick.[5] The church was legally organized on July 1, 1805, at a meeting held at the home of Dr. Hackaliah Burt. In 1810, William Bostwick, one of the principal landowners of the new village, gave an acre of land to the growing congregation and a small frame church was erected in 1811. The building committee was composed of Bostwick, Burt, and Ebenezer Phelps.

The church had four windows on each side, the interior was painted white and was heated with a large stove in the south wall, "part of which was in the body of the church, and part in the vestibule." It "had four large pews occupied by Judge Miller, Mr. [Ebenezer] Phelps, our own [Dill] family, and Mr. Bostwick and his thirteen children."[6] The musi-

---

[4] John Rudd, *Historical Sketch of St. Peter's Church*, 1833.

[5] In 1803 George III was King of England, Thomas Jefferson was President of the United States, and Napoleon had conquered most of Europe. In 1803 the United States made the Louisiana Purchase. In July 1805 the King was still on the throne, Jefferson was still president, Napoleon had been crowned Emperor, and Horatio Nelson was preparing for the Battle of Trafalgar.

[6] Deborah Dill Bronson [Mrs. Parliament Bronson], "Recollections of My Early Life in Auburn," March 8, 1881. *Collections of Cayuga County Historical Society.*

St. Peter's Church was consecrated on August 22, 1812.
It was the first church in the Village of Auburn.

ical Bostwicks were the choir, and the hymn was begun with Mr. Bostwick's pitch pipe.

What was Auburn like and who, more precisely, were these early founders? Why was the name of St. Peter's chosen? Several accounts of early life in the village give us a partial picture of the neighborhood where the church was built and some characterization of the founding families.

William Bostwick was of Scottish descent and was born near Stratford, Connecticut in 1765, as was Hannah his wife. With six of their children they moved from Whitestown in Oneida County to Aurelius [later Auburn] in February 1799. Mr. Bostwick had purchased a one hundred acre square of land which began on the southeast corner of the great Lot No. 46, and was roughly 700 yards in length on each of its four sides. The area extended west on Genesee Street from the present intersection at North and South Streets to the top of the Genesee Street hill. Its width was from Clark Street to south of Fort Hill. The first home of the Bostwicks was a log house on the north side of Genesee Street. In 1803 they built a frame house at the west corner of Genesee and Exchange which in 1804 became a tavern, an inn for strangers, with a long room for village gatherings. In 1816 the Bostwicks moved to a new house on the west corner of Genesee and James, the site of the modern post office. James Street existed then merely as a cowpath that ran toward the creek, the present outlet.

Mr. Bostwick sometimes conducted Sunday services in his home, or occasionally under a large tree. He is remembered as a short, stout man, with musical talent. All of his thirteen children became communicants in their time, and formed the chief source of the music and singing in the small church. His oldest son, William Warner Bostwick, possessed of "a tremendous bass voice," became an Episcopal priest.[7]

Part of the Bostwick household consisted of two black slaves, Sybil, a "superior cook," and Eleven, her husband. Their son George lived with Nathaniel Garrow, Esq., just a short way west, and their daughter Flora worked for Mrs. E. T. Throop.[8]

Bostwick's concern, as he developed his acreage, was to make his portion of the new community a desirable area in which to purchase and settle. Market Street, the location of Major Compston and Colonel Hardenberg, was a narrow lane, which, beginning at a bridge, led up the East Hill to an area attractive in its elevation above the stream. In contrast, much of Bostwick's land was rather casually drained. A deep ravine ran north about where the old Post Office now stands and a pond was near the present Episcopal parish house. But Bostwick succeeded in drawing the center of gravity of the developing village across the creek and into his properties by donating sites for the county court house and the new bank. And in March of 1810 he gave an acre of land further west on Genesee Street for the construction of Auburn's first church, St. Peter's. Thus he improved his holdings with three institutions of civic establishment, court, bank, and church.

In 1791 Robert Dill purchased part of Lot No. 37, substantially the north-west corner of Auburn, an area which began at the western end

---

[7] William Bostwick was known as a talented orchardist, and his son, the Rev. William W. Bostwick, first introduced grape vines to the Finger Lakes region in 1829 by planting them in the rectory garden in Hammondsport to make sacramental wine for his parishes.

[8] Azuba Terry Hunt [Mrs. S. Bronson Hunt], *Collections of Cayuga County Historical Society*, No. 6 (1888), 109.

of Bostwick's holdings. Sometime after 1795 the Dill family, including son John and daughter Caroline, moved from Rome in Oneida County, and established their first home at the intersection of old Franklin Street and Seminary Avenue, where their second daughter Deborah was born in 1808. In 1809 Robert Dill built a new home on the north-east corner of Genesee and Washington, known from its hill-top location as "Mount House." Washington Street was then called Dill's Lane and led down to a Dill factory with its dam and forges. Orchard Street led to an orchard at the rear of the Bostwick home and lot.

On the other side of the road from the Dill house a deep woods extended from in front of St. Peter's Church, all the way west to Nathaniel Garrow's home at the bottom of the Genesee Street hill. Beyond Garrow's handsome home with its cultivated gardens was a toll gate. At the time the church was built the neighborhood was very sparsely populated. Between the Dill's "Mount House" and St. Peter's there were only four houses, one of them the home of the Terry family, who sent their girls to the church. It is to Azuba Terry that we are indebted for a description of the area and its residents. In time a small brick district school was erected on the west side of the church grounds.

Doctor Hackaliah Burt was born in Bridgefield, Connecticut, in 1773. He studied medicine, though later observers were of the opinion that "physic and surgery does not appear to have been congenial to his taste." Whether he ever practiced medicine in Auburn is in question, as he was primarily concerned with the purchase and sale of land, and with the operation of a store. Tall and angular, at the age of twenty-three he came to Auburn in March of 1796, "led by adventure to a place of half a dozen families, the abode of savages."[9] Here he established a

---

[9] Henry Hall, *The History of Auburn* (Auburn, 1869), 537.

mercantile business by which he sold supplies to the Indians who formed a large share of his trade. In 1802 he brought his wife, the former Eunice Howe, to Auburn, and purchased a large "farm" of a hundred acres on the east side of South Street. On its north border he laid out Grover Street. Its south border extended to Swift Street and its east border seems to have been near the outlet. In 1813 he built a home at 51 South Street. Dr. Burt had united with the Episcopal Church at the age of sixteen and was known as a "staunch" Episcopalian. A pillar of St. Peter's, he greatly amused little Azuba Terry when it came to the way he dragged out the refrain of the Litany, which he rendered, as she recalled, as "Lord, h- a- a- ve mer - cy upon us miserable sinners."

Robert Muir came from his native Scotland at age sixteen in 1806, to clerk for a merchant in Auburn. In 1822 he married Nancy Bennett of Auburn and five years later he became an associate of Nathaniel Garrow, George B. Throop, and Eleazar Hill in the manufacture of cotton cloth at Throopsville. Later he operated a dry goods and produce store on Genesee Street's north side, just west of the bridge. Though born a Presbyterian he was an active supporter of St. Peter's, contributing significantly to the church until his financial collapse in 1841.

Ebenezer Phelps owned lands in Cato in 1808 and lived in Sennett in 1827 where his home was the site of the first meeting of the Town of Sennett. Mr. Phelps was one of the original pewholders of St. Peter's first church.

Judge Elijah Miller, also an original pewholder, will be discussed at length later. His position and influence gave further testimony to the importance of the new church. His daughters Lizette and Frances and his sisters Patty and Clara were usually seated in his pew. The independent Lizette was observed to remove her large Leghorn hat in church to rearrange her dark chestnut curls.

Services in the church were a cold affair in winter. The stoves gave insufficient warmth, in spite of the pipes which ran thru the body of the room. Footstoves, filled with glowing coals by the sexton, were delivered noiselessly to the pews of their owners. Large muffs served the ladies as hand warmers and the children for pillows as they endured long sermons and services. But the endurance was made tolerable by the fashions that could be observed. The girls waited to see what the elegant Mrs. E. T. Throop, born Evelina Vredenburgh, would have for a new winter costume or what stunning dress would be worn by one of Judge Miller's family. The Miller daughters introduced the first calling cards to village society, and the Judge was the host for many of the notable entertainments in the locality. The portly judge's negro servant Pete was the favorite master of ceremonies at all the balls and gatherings for young and old. In the last years of the frame church one could catch a glimpse of William Seward's sister, petite and lady-like, with "hair like ruby wine."[10] Attending Sunday service at St. Peter's had more interest than just what the Prayer Book provided.

And why was the church dedicated as St. Peter's? The most likely reason is that it was taken from several other prominent churches in the areas familiar to its founders, especially St. Peter's, Albany. There is also a certain hegemonic tone to the name of the first among the Apostles, he to whom were specifically entrusted the Keys of the Kingdom. The name was possibly designed to set the Presbyterians on notice.

---

[10] Azuba Terry Hunt, *idem*, 107.

The first Episcopal clergy to arrive in Aurelius were lonely missionaries who traveled about the sparsely settled parts of the state, and while today we may list them as "Rector of St. Peter's," the reality was that these early itinerants, the Rev. Davenport Phelps, the Rev. William A. Clarke, Dr. Daniel McDonald and the Rev. W. H. Northrop[11] were ministering to a number of missionary stations in the area. Davenport Phelps had his residence in Geneva. Dr. McDonald, a classics scholar born at Watertown, Connecticut, in 1785, signed himself modestly, "Resident Presbyter of Aurelius." These worthies, beginning in the year 1803, made use of a register book begun either by Davenport Phelps or William Bostwick, which forms St. Peter's Parish Register Number One. They recorded baptisms made in Aurelius, Camillus, Skaneateles, Marcellus, and Brutus. Bishop John H. Hobart confirmed twenty-four people at St. Peter's in 1815, six men and eighteen women, but since the total number of <u>local</u> communicants in 1817 was only thirty (including Jenny, "black servant to Mrs. Cumpston"), it is obvious that some of the twenty-four came to Aurelius that day from other settlements.

For the period 1803 to 1823, the first twenty years of the congregation's existence, in part with no church edifice, the parish record reveals an association led by laymen, with little business to conduct save the annual elections. The first wardens were village pioneers William Bostwick and William J. Hardenbergh. "After each celebration of the Communion the silver service was carried home by either Dr. Burt or

---

[11] In 1816 Azuba Terry went to recite her catechism to Mr. Northrup, whom she describes as a Carolinian, "of great piety, quite young, and of delicate and refined organization." His health, affected by Auburn's climate, compelled his return to his native place, and he died shortly thereafter. Azuba Terry Hunt, *idem*, 107.

the Bostwicks."[12] The congregation enjoyed the services of an itinerant clergy who were paid in part as missionaries of the Diocese of New York and in part from local contributions. The record of baptisms, confirmations, marriages, and burials is therefore understandably fragmentary. What we can determine from the recorded numbers is that in the fifteen years between 1803 and 1818 there were 154 baptisms, or about ten per year, and that in the five years, 1819 to 1823, there were 101 baptisms, or about twenty per year. Not only was the village growing in population, but in those five years from 1819 to 1823, the church had the services of a more resident clergyman, in the person of the Rev. Lucius Smith.[13] Smith, a former Lieutenant Colonel in the Connecticut militia during the War of 1812, was a hospitable and sociable man whose talents were subsequently appreciated by the academy at Geneva and he was asked to take on additional work as a traveling agent for the school.

This dual responsibility seems to have worked for a time, but soon the obvious needs and resources of the growing village made the vestry feel that Mr. Smith's talents should be kept closer to home. In January of 1823 when he sought leave of the vestry to engage as agent for Geneva Academy, the vestry stipulated that he must provide ministers for any Sunday absences. A sporadic schedule of services was no longer to be tolerated. At the annual meeting on the Monday of Easter Week, in late March 1823, Smith presided over an apparently tranquil gathering of

---

[12] Deborah Dill Bronson, "Recollections..."

[13] Azuba Terry remembered Smith as hospitable to a fault, fond of children's games, always cheerful. One source of that cheer may have been bottled, as she comments, "What, though he had some taint of moral weakness, as who has not, yet may God remember him in mercy, for his truly generous nature made him a friend to all." Azuba Terry Hunt, *idem*, 115.

communicants and pew-holders. On June 30, 1823 at a special meeting of the vestry, with Smith presiding, it was moved by Dr. Hackaliah Burt that Mr. Smith be 'disengaged' as rector, effective October first, and that they get another rector. When someone moved that such a decision be postponed, the vote, with Burt opposed, was divided, three to three, and Smith cast a deciding vote in favor of postponement. However by August 21, 1823, Smith sent in his letter of resignation. Dated Geneva, July 21, 1823, it read, in part:

> Gentlemen, after mature deliberation, I am convinced that there is no reasonable prospect that any reconciliation will take place on the part of the individual who is particularly dissatisfied with me as Rector and believing that my own happiness and comfort is connected with a dissolution...I leave you gentlemen not as your Enemy but as your Friend,
>
> Lucius Smith

The part played by 'the individual,' without question Hackaliah Burt, must be noted. With William Bostwick ailing, Burt was at that moment and for a long time the only surviving member of the vestry from the earliest days of organization. A founding member, and Warden from 1805 until 1834, zealous for the welfare of the parish, Dr. Burt continued to make problems for the clergy. The lawyers on the vestry, George B. Throop, Enos T. Throop, William H. Seward and others, appeared to be open to compromise in any disagreements, but the doctor of medicine, Hackaliah Burt, wanted his way and only his way. It was he, for instance, who moved in 1827 that any burials in the churchyard be restricted to supporting members and their families.[14]

---

[14] Vestry Minutes, September 6, 1827.

After Mr. Smith left there was a brief interval in which two recently ordained deacons filled in, Burton Hickox and Osamus J. Smith.[15] Dr. McDonald occasionally came over from Geneva to help out. But permanence, a resident rector, was needed in the growing village. The congregation, with no regular shepherd, was described as in a "desponding state." To further establish the parish, William Bostwick, near his life's end, promised to give another lot on which to build a rectory.

In this frame of things the vestry decide to call a full time rector. They chose a native of Easton, Pennsylvania, the Rev. Samuel Sitgreaves, Jr., the well-favored son of a wealthy jurist and congressman.

Samuel Sitgreaves, Jr., was born in April of 1779, attended Princeton for a time, and at the mature age of 33 began to study for the ministry with Bishop William White in Philadelphia. In 1820 at forty-one he was ordained deacon and three years later he was made priest in August of 1823. In December of 1823 he married Anne Lyman, and in mid 1824 he accepted the position of rector of St. Peter's, Auburn.

It was a great error on the part of the pampered and newly-wedded man of forty-five. The vestry promised him a rectory to live in, but waited for the gift of a building site that William Bostwick had promised to donate. The city-bred couple were forced to live in hired quarters. Auburn's cold weather disagreed with them. The society of Auburn was "tolerable pleasant" but far from the polished Philadelphia to which they were accustomed. Childless Anne Sitgreaves had no friends of her own sort, and lacking a home in which to keep house, forced herself to

---

[15] They both signed themselves, "Deacon officiating at Auburn."

reading and music and visiting. She wept when Samuel was away even for a few hours.[16]

When William Bostwick died in 1825,[17] the "handsome lot" which he was to give to the church for the promised parsonage was found to be "altogether too small & that it was encumbered with unreasonable conditions." Thus Samuel Sitgreaves, Jr. informed his uncle Jackson Kemper in Philadelphia and added, "that we were put to a complete standstill."[18] As the 1825 building season advanced and material prices shot up under the pressure of the twenty-one new houses being constructed in Auburn that summer, a parsonage for the rector and his unhappy wife seemed further and further off. They traveled back and forth to eastern Pennsylvania, with the result that the Rev. Mr. Sitgreaves spent less and less time in Auburn, openly longing to exchange his post for another.

He was neither a keeper of good records[19] nor an ardent pastor. The vestry's hope to maintain resident clerical services for the parish faded. The enthusiasm that prompted so many generous parishioners to make subscriptions to the 'rectory of the future' slowly diminished.

---

[16] Samuel Sitgreaves, Jr. to Jackson Kemper, August 22, [1825], Kemper Papers, Madison, Wisconsin.

[17] The tablet above Bostwick's grave, in the churchyard's present Throop enclosure, reads, "To the memory of William Bostwick, who departed this life in the peace of the Christian, June 24, 1825, aged fifty-nine."

[18] Sitgreaves to Kemper, *idem*.

[19] For example, the record of the marriage of Frances Miller to William H. Seward is not to be found in the parish register of the church but in the pages of the *Cayuga Republican*, October 27, 1824, "married Oct. 20, 1824, Wednesday am, at St. Peter's Church by Rev. Mr. Setgreaves [sic]."

From Tavern

In July of 1826 there arrived in Auburn an experienced Episcopal clergyman of proven pastoral abilities, who had come to New York's 'Wild West' for his health and to take on the light work of supervising the little Auburn Academy. The Rev. John Churchill Rudd, D.D., had been rector in Elizabethtown, New Jersey, for twenty years when his health broke and he decided to move to the healthier west to seek the improvement of his 'rheumatic difficulty.'[20]

Like Samuel Sitgreaves, John Rudd too came from a distinguished family. A month younger than Mr. Sitgreaves, he was a native of Norwich, Connecticut, descended on his mother's side from the Huntingtons. In 1803 the Rev. John Henry Hobart officiated at Rudd's marriage to Phebe Eliza Russell. Their home in Elizabeth was renowned for its hospitality and Mrs. Rudd's cooking. When they moved to Auburn, accompanied by two of their children, they had been married for twenty-three years.

Sitgreaves immediately took advantage of the opportunity to unload the clerical work of the parish on the compliant Rudd. From the arrival of John Rudd's family of four in July of 1826 until Sitgreaves' resignation in December of that year, the unhappy rector was present for only two Sundays. Rudd took the services on all the rest.

---

[20] 1826, July 17, "On this day I arrived in Auburn to take charge of the Auburn Academy, the Rev. Mr. Sitgreaves, the Rector, being absent, I was requested to officiate for him – this I did with the exception of two Sundays when he was present until Dec. 2nd, 1826, when he having resigned the Rectorship I was appointed and entered upon my duties the following day. In order that the register may be more useful and convenient it will during my Rectorship be arranged in different divisions. J. C. Rudd. " Parish Register 1.

There was some excuse. The Hon. Samuel Sitgreaves, the father, was on his deathbed in Easton, and passed away in April of 1827. The son was needed at home to manage the substantial fortune and affairs of the family.

But, family obligations or not, Sam Sitgreaves obviously had no inclination for the pastoral ministry. According to the parish register, in his entire two years or so in Auburn, he performed two weddings, presented no one for confirmation, and baptized and buried one sick child whose father later had himself to record the event in the parish register![21]

When Sitgreaves resigned, writing from Easton on November 9, 1826, the vestry accepted his decision and a committee composed of Enos Throop, the future governor, and the ever-present Hackaliah Burt tendered him the customary departing written testimonial. Dr. Rudd was made rector and given a salary retroactive to October 18.

With the rectorship of John Rudd the parish's fortunes rapidly advanced. Confirmations resumed, twenty-one in 1826, fifteen in 1828, nine in 1830, administered by Rudd's friend, Bishop John Henry Hobart. In seven years of ministry Rudd baptized 114 persons.

The baptisms administered by Dr. Rudd bear witness to the increasing availability of the church's ministrations in the new village. Often whole families would take the opportunity to catch up with years of neglect

---

[21] Register 1, [Entry for the baptism of Sarah Gridley 15 months old, daughter of General Gridley, October 1824], "The above entry was made by General Gridley after my Rectorship and is stated by various persons to be the only baptism administered by Mr. Sitgreaves during the three years of ministry here!!!" [in Rudd's handwriting.]

and would be baptized together, especially when the nearness of death impelled them to serious thoughts. One characteristic case can be seen in the family of Erastus Humphreys, a doctor of medicine. Dr. Humphreys had been listed as a communicant on November 4, 1827, but it was not until July 13, 1828 that he, his wife Anna [Ann], and daughter Laura Ann were baptized. Rudd noted of Laura Ann that she was "their daughter on sick bed and probably near her end in consumption." Mrs. Fosgate, Mrs. Rudd, and Miss S. Fosgate went to the home with the rector to serve as witnesses. Laura Ann was buried nine days later on July 22, 1828, aged twenty-two, united to her parents in holy baptism. On September 21st, in connection with the bishop's visitation, the rest of the Humphreys children were baptized in church, George, aged 13; Frederick, 11; Martha Adeline [Mary Angeline?], 6; Chloe Cornelia, 4; and Helen Ann, 2. The following day, September 22, 1828, Dr. Humphreys, his wife Ann and another family member, Emmaline Humphreys, were confirmed by Bishop Hobart.

And at last some element of ministerial permanence was assured to the parish by the purchase of a rectory, a "parsonage house." A brick home on a large lot just to the east of the church was purchased in late 1828 for $2200 and the Rudds moved in. Rudd had already begun the publication of the *Gospel Messenger*, a periodical which he was to write and manage for many years.[22] The printing of the weekly, devoted to current issues as well as to devotional materials, took place in a small brick house just to the west of the churchyard.

The *Gospel Messenger* began publication on January 20, 1827, as "The Church Record of Western New York." "…Nearly every intelligent

---

[22] There were 66 periodicals published in the state of New York in 1810. By 1840 the number rose to over 200.

Church family took it in as if it were their daily bread, and read it from end to end." "Dr. Rudd was not a forcible original writer, but he had a rare faculty of selection…which made the paper always interesting as well as profitable."[23] A good portion of Rudd's time was devoted to the weekly publication.

The new rectory became a sort of 'Episcopal inn,' a dwelling to which church members repaired on their journeys through Auburn, its lighted windows a source of reassurance to passersby on the turnpike to the west. Mrs. Rudd, previously adept at preparing meals over an open fire in the fireplace, was soon provided with a cookstove. Dr. Rudd continued to teach in the academy. His sermons were appreciated. In 1828 Frances Seward informed her absent husband William that she had heard a "good sermon from Dr. Rudd this afternoon."[24]

In 1830 the rectory gained new and tragic importance. In its upper chambers the devoted churchman John Henry Hobart breathed his last. On an episcopal visitation to western New York, the energetic Bishop of New York passed away in the home of his devoted friend and adviser. Hobart and Rudd had been close for years.

His solemn funeral in New York City was attended by, among many others, the Governor of the State of New York, St. Peter's own vestryman Enos Throop. Hobart's friends and admirers commissioned a marble bust to be carved by the sculptor John Frazee, to be sent to

---

[23] Charles Wells Hayes, *The Diocese of Western New York, History and Recollections* (Rochester, 1905), 69.
[24] Frances Miller Seward to William H. Seward, Oct. 13, 1828. Frances Miller Seward Collection, Rush Rhees Library, University of Rochester. [Hereafter, FMS to WHS, Oct. 13, 1828.]

Auburn and mounted in St. Peter's Church with an accompanying monumental tablet.

An improved John Rudd confidently planned a trip to England in 1831. "Good sermon from Dr. Rudd. He is going to England in the spring. S. Hulbert was here to collect money to purchase a new cloak for Mrs. Rudd. Silly, they called on a number who I am sure cannot afford cloaks for themselves."[25]

The Rudds gave a party.[26] But not everyone approved of entertainment. "Mrs. Rudd's party created a great schism in the church. J—— and his hounds are going to withdraw on acct. of his wife being neglected. Dr. Rudd is very much censured for his extravagant panegyrics about Dr. Morgan's practice."[27]

Later she reported, "The Fosgates[28] do not attend church anymore. They have become displeased and dissatisfied with Dr. and Mrs. Rudd because they do not visit them and they were not invited to Mrs. Rudd's party."[29] Dr. Rudd struck Mrs. Fosgate's name from the

---

[25] FMS to WHS, Jan. 2, 1831.
[26] FMS to WHS, Jan. 12, 1831.
[27] FMS to WHS, Feb. 7, 1831.
[28] The *Skaneateles Telegraph*, January, March, April 1830, carried an advertisement for Dr. Blanchard Fosgate's "B. Fosgate's Anodyne Cordial" with this testimony by Col. W. H. Seward, "I believe it to be a valuable medicine for the purpose for which it is recommended." It was intended for "diseases of the breast and lungs, and bowel afflictions, diarrhea, dysentery."
[29] FMS to WHS, Mar.11, 1831.

communicant list, with the notation "considered as removed," i.e., moved away.³⁰

And from the village's major denomination the morals of the lively rector drew criticism. "Dr. Rudd was accused by a [Presbyterian] seminary student of dancing at the New Year's Ball, and asked to contradict it." He was "asked if he had not gone to Mrs. Seward's party where they had fiddling and dancing." An incensed Frances Seward concluded to retaliate by not attending any more Presbyterian meetings.³¹

Delayed in its execution, the Hobart monument, shipped late in the season from New York to Auburn by canal packet, was held up somewhere on the frozen Erie Canal in the winter of 1831-1832.

The wood frame St. Peter's Church had been enlarged in 1831 at an expense of $1300, with a new organ and bell. Frances Seward reported that she attended services in the newly enclosed church in late September of 1831, and that though the new arrangement struck her as "low and long" the church was well filled.³²

The frame church was heated by two 'box' stoves, low flat iron boxes capable of burning logs four feet in length. These devices were peculiarly placed with one end in the enclosed vestibule and the other projecting into the church proper through an opening in the wall. Perhaps this was so that they could be stoked from the vestibule without

---

[30] Later, the Rev. Mr. Lucas restored her name to the communicant list with the notation "Returned to the Communion. Mrs. Fosgate had <u>voluntarily</u> withdrawn herself for some years."
[31] FMS to WHS, Mar. 7, 1831.
[32] FMS to WHS, Sept. 25, 1831.

interrupting the liturgy. One could peer over the surface of the stoves and gain a view of the interior of the church. It was in this manner that young William Seward first spied his future bride, Miss Frances Miller, as he came to St. Peter's Church seeking her father Elijah on a Christmas Sunday morning in 1823.

On the cold night of February 5, 1832, this arrangement overheated and caught the church on fire. The recently enlarged building was pitifully destroyed, new improvements, new organ, and new bell, all lost in flames. The shock to the congregation was enormous. For the first and saddest of many times, Auburn's Episcopalians shifted their worship to the nearby county courthouse.

> A meeting of the parishioners was held the day following the fire, to consider the condition of the parish, and see what could be done to repair the loss. The late Judge [Joseph F.] Richardson was made chairman of the meeting. After considerable discussion as to the loss sustained and the debt upon the church for the late improvements, Judge Richardson, in his characteristic emphatic manner, said: 'We have not convened to talk over the loss of the church and the bell and the organ, or what the parish is owing. All this we knew before. But we have come to build a new church. If someone will draw a subscription paper, I will sign $500.' This was done at once, and his munificent subscription was at once followed by several for a like amount, among whom were Dr. Burt, Judge Miller, George B. Throop, Hiram Bostwick, and Robert Muir...and by Capt. William Swain...[33]

---

[33] John Brainard, *The History of St. Peter's Church...* (Auburn, 1888.), 37.

With such determination by the congregation and Dr. Rudd, and aided substantially by the generosity of St. Peter's friends throughout the state, a new church of stone was erected on the same spot, and consecrated by Bishop Benjamin Onderdonk on August 8, 1833, just a year and a half later. The Hobart monument, miraculously preserved from fiery ruin as it lay safe in its packing crates locked in on the frozen canal, was placed in a niche in the west rear of the chancel wall.

The dollar cost of the new stone church was just under $10,000, some of which was pledged by prominent members and some was provided by a mortgage taken on the parsonage. The human cost was great as well. John Rudd, seldom a well man, was burdened with the responsibility of promoting the construction, and was sent all over the eastern part of the state to solicit contributions. On his journeys he raised about a thousand dollars from individuals and communities, and obtained the promise of $2500 from Trinity Church, New York, to be paid on completion of the construction.[34]

The vestry, stressed by the task and weighed down by the debt they had contracted, began to scrutinize Rudd's fundraising accounts in a manner that surely irritated him. In January of 1833 they asked him for a detailed reckoning of all the money he had raised. He complied. They refused to accept his notations and returned his figures to him for clarification, demanding that he turn over to them all letters that indicated the amounts he had received or been promised, especially the resolution of Trinity Church which referred to the grant of the $2500. He complied again on February 8, carefully reporting everything, including the $4.96 he had received for the melted bell.

---

[34] A marble plaque commemorating this gift hangs in the present tower entrance to the church.

From Tavern

As a further blow to Rudd, the vestry, shepherding their resources, rescinded their month-old decision to allow Rudd and James Bostwick, the young organist, to raise funds to buy a new organ. The February minutes hint of the vestry's growing estrangement from Rudd.

On March 14, 1833, Rudd resigned. From 1831 he had experienced factions in the parish, much stress, and all this while he was in poor health. The vestry voted to settle with him for his salary to the first of April.

Rudd's letter of resignation cited as the reasons for his resignation that he was occupied with his weekly publication which he could not abandon, that he had had health disruptions, and that he was weary from the "exertions of last year." Over the trying years he had attended to the interment of an esteemed minister of the congregation [Dr. McDonald], had suffered the calamity of a church in flames, and had witnessed "the departure of a Venerated Prelate whose monument is to adorn your new Temple."[35]

"This, added to the present exceedingly excited state of the religious community, requiring a great increase of parochial attention," was too much for Rudd. Telling the vestry that he would continue to minister as best he could until September, it is obvious that, tired, a bit strained, and aware of dissension in the parish, John Rudd wanted release from the responsibility. In his time of ministry he had not only performed a great task, but had had to deal with members who had become negative toward him. Even after he resigned, and the vestry invited him to continue to preach he was sometimes shown marked discourtesy. "Mrs. Smith was there and when the Dr. rose to preach she took her children

---

[35] Vestry Minutes, Book 1, March 14, 1833.

and withdrew, walking down the whole length of the aisle – did you ever see anything to equal this woman?"[36] When Rudd still preached occasionally in late 1834, Mrs. Seward reported that her aunt Clary was very much disappointed in the fact, and that "Muir left the church."[37]

The vestry continued to dispute money matters with him. As late as January of 1834 when Hiram Bostwick moved that Rudd was owed $330 for additional services up until May 1833, the motion was voted down, with Hackaliah Burt leading the refusal.

With the new stone church consecrated on August 5, 1833,[38] Rudd, the editor, the writer, got in the last word. He summed up the progress of St. Peter's congregation since he took over and published it in the *Gospel Messenger* as part of a history of the church. He appended an extract from the same to the first sermon he preached in the new stone church, a work which he then published in September, 1833.[39]

---

[36] FMS to WHS, August 12, 1833. Mrs. Smith and husband were also in arrears in their pew rentals. Vestry minutes of June 8, 1835 and June 9, 1837.

[37] FMS to WHS, December 21, 1834.

[38] Frances, who characteristically liked the old church better, reported to her husband that she had gone to the consecration of the new church. "Bishop Onderdonk and 4 or 5 of the most common looking men performed the ceremony." She noted that there was an excellent sermon and that the church was filled, principally by women. "The pews are very high and uncomfortable…the drapings of the pulpit in very bad taste…was it before you went away that they surmounted each point of the tower of the church with a golden ball – unsuited to the architecture?" FMS to WHS, August 5, 1833.

[39] "A Sermon Preached in St. Peter's Church, Auburn, The Tenth Sunday After Trinity, August 11, 1833," by John C. Rudd.

> The smallness of the congregation in 1826…could hardly be expected to be followed by the results of the subsequent year…the purchasing of a Parsonage House and garden very pleasantly and appropriately located, adjoining the church yard.
>
> Adult baptisms by the writer…34 — infants 80 — total 114…additions to the communion [communicants] by the writer…were 60, and by removals [transfers] to the place 34 — making the additions 94. In the same time the losses of communicants by death and removal from the place have been 37.
>
> The marriages … have been 35. — The interments of the same time in the cemetery of St. Peter's have been 42, and 24 attended in other yards… The number of attendants upon…services has increased in the last seven years in a ratio of 5 to 1, while the population of the village has in the same time advanced … little more than one fourth.

And Rudd pointed out that in good weather the attendance at service grew from 50 to 150, and that Sundays with over 250 worshippers had been frequent in the last two years. The frame church had been enlarged to seat these numbers, he reminded his readers, and the larger stone church built after the fire was a response to the growth that had taken place during his ministry.

Leaving Auburn, Rudd moved the *Gospel Messenger* to Utica, where he lived until his death at 69 in 1848. The 'charming, hospitable' Phebe returned to live in Auburn and was buried by Dr. Brainard on October 7, 1867, aged 88.

When Rudd had submitted his resignation on March 14, 1833, the congregation, as it had done since the fire, was still worshipping in the Court House. The vestry, wasting no time, called the Rev. Mr. Tiffany of Cooperstown, promising him that they would likely be in their new stone church by June first, and that they were anxious to fill the position quickly, for "a very extraordinary religious excitement has prevailed in this place the last six or eight weeks which in our opinion renders it peculiarly necessary and important that our congregation should enjoy the constant services of a clergyman." The vestry were obviously hoping to combine the advantage of the new stone church with something similar to Rudd's regular ministration and sound counsel from which the congregation had prospered for the previous seven years.

But Mr. Tiffany stayed in Cooperstown. The vestry, gaining experience, invited the Rev. Thomas S. Brittan of New York to come for a visit of two or three weeks to look over the parish. They liked him, called him, and nevertheless failed to raise enough salary money. Mr. Brittan stayed in New York.

What was this 'extraordinary religious excitement' that so concerned the vestry in the spring of 1833? It was the disturbance engendered by the new revival methods of Charles G. Finney and his followers. Against such waves of spiritual fever the vestry knew that it was important to have a regular rector on the scene to deal with the unsettling excitement. They needed a spiritual leader to preserve church doctrine against the storms of enthusiasm, to lead beside still waters such sheep as might be tempted to stray. The calm faith and practice of the Episcopal Church was severely challenged by this new approach to Christian commitment.

Certainly the fright and insecurity associated with the great cholera epidemic of 1832 still continued to unsettle minds in the isolated village. The deadly mystery of the initial plague of cholera demoralized lowland settlements and hilltop towns alike. Striking first in Quebec, the unfathomable scourge marched on central New York from two directions, down the canal from Buffalo, and up the Hudson and Mohawk rivers. On June 15, 1832 it was in Quebec and Montreal. On June 18 it was in Ogdensburg. On June 21st Governor Enos Throop called a special session of the legislature. On June 26th an Irish immigrant Fitzgerald fell dead of it in New York City.

Persons afflicted were often healthy in the morning, ill at noon, and dead by nightfall. No one knew for a certainty what its cause was, and its victims were mostly the filthy, the hungry, the ignorant. Moralists said it resulted from dangerous habits of intemperance, bad vegetables, wrong food. The majority of a medical profession which was still ignorant of bacteria and germs, pronounced that it was caused by a 'miasma,' something 'atmospheric.' The clergy were sure it was a punishment for sin because it was rampant among the intemperate poor and the immorally crowded.

In isolated rural areas of New York the scourge was stunning, terrifying, when faced alone without the comfort of human company. And the common people grasped that despite the variety in diagnosis by the clergy or the medical theorists, the cholera was — horribly, darkly, mysteriously — contagious. Immigrants who tried to jump ship along the Erie Canal were hurled back onto the packet boats by local militia, and "armed Rhode Islanders turned back New Yorkers fleeing across Long Island Sound."[40]

The revivalist ministers of the day took advantage of the spread of the mysterious disease to drive home their basic point. "Brief life is here our portion… repent while there is time." The lurid descriptions of hell, the urgency of decision, the necessity for individual conversion, here, <u>now</u>, found new substantiation in the unpredictability of sudden death.

The greatest of the revivalists, Charles G. Finney, was no stranger to Auburn. Brought in to preach by the innovative Presbyterian divine, Dirk Lansing, Finney had first harrowed Auburn in 1826, and again in 1831. While Finney himself lay ill with the cholera in New York in 1832-33, his methods and his message still hung over the village. Contrary to the moribund passivity of traditional Calvinism, Finney vividly, graphically, preached that in view of the reality and certainty of hell fire it was necessary to <u>do something</u> to reach out to God, to <u>make</u> a personal decision, to <u>accept</u> Christ, and to <u>act</u> to bring others to the same resolution.

---

[40] Charles E. Rosenberg, *The Cholera Years: The United States in 1832, 1849, and 1866* (Chicago, 1962), 5-37.

Excursus I:
John Rudd Calls for a Parsonage

Reprinted from the *Gospel Messenger*, May 2, 1829, III, p. 62.

(The following address, was delivered before the congregation of St. Peter's church, Auburn, in November last, and though it may be considered of too local a character to interest all, there are probably many of our readers who will not regret its insertion in the Messenger. We are happy to state that the measure contemplated has been so far completed as to allow the Rector to take possession of the property procured, and which proves a very agreeable residence. If the members of the congregation continue their liberal efforts they will soon finish a permanent evidence of their desire for the comfort of their minister, and for the perpetuity of that mode of worship in which ample means are afforded for the correct understanding of the doctrines of the Gospel, and for the encouragement of holiness of heart and life. [Editor, John Rudd, D.D.])

Brethren, — the thought has suggested itself to me that it would not be improper to state to the congregation, some considerations in relation to a late attempt of the Vestry to obtain a Parsonage House and lot, as the property of this Parish. An opportunity has been presented to purchase on very advantageous terms, the property adjoining the Church-yard on the eastern side. The reasons for obtaining a parsonage are surely very obvious, but as they may not engage the attention of all, it will not be amiss to observe, that when a congregation has a comfortable parsonage, they have a security for the permanence of their parish affairs, which no other circumstance of like value can give. In the perpetual fluctuation of human things, no associations suffer more frequently and severely, than small country parishes. An unexpected removal, or an unlooked for death, of a single individual sometimes so weakens the congregation that it becomes almost wholly paralyzed in its efforts. It has always been found that a small stipend for a minister is much more valuable with a permanent parsonage residence than a larger annual salary, when no certain residence is provided. The earlier after a congregation is formed, a property like the one alluded to is secured, the better. As the country and the place advance in age, there will be generally, an advance in property, and of course an increase in difficulty in obtaining the accommodation desired. There are at this moment very many congregations of various denominations in the U.S. who would not be able to have settled ministers but for their having parsonages, which were provided at an early day.

I am well aware there will be a vigorous effort necessary for the accomplishment of the object which your vestry have undertaken, but I am also confident, that there is abundant ability, and I trust I am not mistaken when I say, there is public spirit sufficient here to meet the measure in question. The terms of purchase are such, and the means in part provided are such, that with the ordinary blessing of providence, no very great individual sacrifice need be made, if all would enter unitedly into the undertaking. — Yours is, I know, a comparatively new congregation, it has been obliged to struggle with very many difficulties, and has fluctuated much, and been often deeply depressed while the great burthen has fallen on a few. A better day seems to have dawned upon your prospects. Many of you, it is true, cannot have all the attachments to the church that those longer acquainted with her, may be supposed to cherish, but from all the opportunities I have had for judging, and from the personal kindness I have experienced since my residence among you, I am persuaded you all desire the prosperity and permanence of this Parish. In forming this opinion, let me ask, can any one measure be better calculated to secure this point than that of completing the undertaking proposed? Living as you do in a rapidly improving country, prospered as you have been, and increasing in the good things of this life, as I hope, and am happy to believe you are, can it be esteemed by you any great hardship to put your united efforts to this matter, and at once to say, let the thing *be done*? Will not every one of you derive gratification from reflecting hereafter, that you had a share in the work which will stand as a lasting monument of the liberality of this people? Will it not gratify your posterity to know that you were honorable contributors to a measure which has done good to the cause of the Christian Church? Is there one of your descendants, think you, who will love your memory the less for what you do in this matter, and can you leave them a better legacy than a provision that they may enjoy the preached Gospel? Your riches they may misapply, love is a gift that they cannot spend. Again, a parsonage house is a bond of union, in a parish it is a kind of center where every member of the congregation feels himself at home, and this feeling, whenever he calls there to see the family of his minister, or to consult him on matters of the highest importance, becomes an increasing bond of union, and it is thus that a spirit of general harmony may be promoted.

I am aware my brethren, that in urging this upon you, I subject myself to the charge of being influenced by selfish motives, and that I am pleading the cause of my own accommodation. Tho' I will not pretend that I have not selfish feelings, as well as other men, still I will deny that these feelings ever have induced me to urge a step in the affairs of the Church, with a view to my own advantage, and I will say here in this sacred place, that did you know the history of my life, and of my ministry, you would every one of you, be satisfied that my declaration is correct. I should no doubt be befitted by the measure but how long

From Tavern

is it probable I could enjoy that benefit? At my time of life, and suffering under some severe pressures of anxiety and disease, I ought not to calculate strongly upon any earthly possessions or comforts. At present, we are I believe harmoniously united & I have surely many reasons to be grateful for the kindness and respect that I have enjoyed among you. That this harmony will continue will be my effort & my prayers, but rest assured, the first moment that I discover the threat of any disruption of the friendship now prevailing, I must and will retire from your desk and pulpit. — But while we are happily united, and may this unity long continue, I must urge upon you every measure which I am convinced will benefit you, your children and your parish. Here my brethren I must leave this subject. You will, I doubt not, give due weight to my remarks, and you will do your duty by yourselves, by the Church and by your God; and may his spirit be your guide.

Excursus II:
Hobart Churchmanship versus
  the Second Great Awakening

On August 11, 1833, the Tenth Sunday after Trinity, the Rev. Dr. John Churchill Rudd preached the first sermon delivered after the consecration of the new stone St. Peter's Church. Rudd had resigned as rector of the church in order to devote full time to the publication of the weekly *Gospel Messenger*, and in so doing to escape from the tensions of pastoral responsibility.

But the prevailing "extraordinary religious excitement" of the current phase of the Second Great Awakening which raged through the streets and Protestant assemblies of Auburn, and the contrast of the dedication of a second, larger, "Gothic," Episcopal church in stone, afforded John Rudd an excellent opportunity to lay out some basic tenets of the High Church Episcopalianism which he and the late Bishop John Henry Hobart both vigorously espoused.

The personal background which Rudd brought to the occasion was a recent story of seven wearying years of serving a parish he never intended to shepherd. After twenty productive years in New Jersey, he had come to Auburn to restore his shattered health. From the relatively light work of principal of the Auburn Academy, he had been drafted, due to the absentee rectorship and resignation of the incumbent Samuel Sitgreaves, Jr., into full pastoral responsibility for the neglected parish. His beloved friend Bishop Hobart had died in his care in 1830. After providing leadership for improvements to the frame church next door on Genesee Street, Rudd had watched it burn to the ground on the night of February 5, 1832. He rallied the congregation from this loss, and traveled most of eastern New York, personally collecting a third of the contributions for the new church. After the vestry had inspected his accounts with exasperating exactitude, and even before the new stone church had risen over the ashes of the wooden one, the fifty-four year old Doctor of Divinity had opted to lay down his pastoral burden.

The sermon he preached that August Sunday was the work of a mature, highly intelligent, self-taught cleric who shared the theology of John Henry Hobart as fully as any man alive. Hobart had performed the marriage of John and Phebe Rudd, had been a frequent guest in their rectories for thirty years, and had, ill and far from home, found in their Auburn parsonage the haven in which to spend his final hours. Even as the sermon was delivered the bust of the revered bishop, set upon a monument lovingly inscribed by his admirers, looked down upon the Auburn congregation from the front wall of the new church. Led by Senior Warden Hackaliah Burt, a hard-minded doctor of such medicine as there was in that time and place, the house-proud vestry sat before the pulpit in their paid-up pews.

Outside the continuing effects of the terror that strikes in the noonday, the deadly Cholera Epidemic of 1832, added emphasis to the religious awakening surging through Calvinistic Auburn, spurred on by "New Measure" Presbyterians and the calculated revival techniques of Charles Grandison Finney. In this moment of radical agitation without, and complacent accomplishment within, Rudd put his question.

'Why a church? Why an Episcopal Church? Why a stone permanent Gothic building? Are not the quickened emotions of the individual heart the most important things?'

TO TEMPLE

The preacher took his text from First Peter, the verses in the second chapter about living stones, in which Christ is the living cornerstone, his followers are lively stones, and the stone which the builders rejected is become a stone of stumbling and a rock of offense. St. Peter, Rudd said, was following up the prediction of Isaiah, a contemplation of that coming church of the Redeemer, the "medium through which spiritual intercourse was to be held with God," "the spiritual household in which they are to have communicated to them those gifts and graces of the Holy Ghost which enable them to grow up unto all pleasing in the sight of the Lord."

From the outset of his remarks Rudd asserted the necessity of growth, and progress, of development in the life of the Christian and growth into 'the fullness of stature in Christ Jesus.' "All these expressions," he stated, "imply that advancement in the vigorous growth of the soul in faith and love, which alone can constitute us the true and living members of the body of Christ."

The calculated format of the revival meetings which were the mainstay of the later Awakening depended on 'tabernacle' assemblies of days or a week, in which teams of preachers delivered sermon upon sermon designed to produce, over a few days, a "Conversion" which moved through the formulated stages of "Concern" for one's soul, "Inquiry" as to how to be saved, "Anxiety" over fear of damnation, "Conviction" of one's sins, and "Repentance and Surrender" by self-dedication and change of heart. The "Conversion" which resulted carried with it, as proof of a bestowal of grace, a visible emotional state marked by copious tears and frantic concern for the salvation of family and friends. Salvation was to be furthered along by an act of the will, a decision in personal faith, followed by devoted service. The emotional revivals of the day, outcroppings of a popular, grass-roots culture which was challenging and displacing hierarchies and old orders of power, had their parallels in western New York in the anti-Masonic revolt, and, as the medical profession proved impotent in the face of epidemics like cholera, also could be felt in the growth of nostrums and alternative health practices.

By the 1830's an "Evangelical Empire," an empire of benevolent activities which crossed denominational lines, had created major organizations like the American Bible Society, the American Tract Society, and the American Sunday School Union. These interdenominational societies with their implied claim to a national mandate cranked out millions of pages of literature each month. Their formidable mass of blurred Protestantism challenged the distinctiveness of the minority Episcopal Church. The broad views of the American Bible Society had been anathema to Bishop Hobart, who started his own Church version in New York. To combat the publications of the tract and Sunday School societies, John Rudd had founded the *Gospel Messenger*, a weekly paper whose ecclesiology was drawn directly from Hobart.

With a view to the revivals' apparent opposition to Church principles, Rudd made clear his claim. "Christ," he said, "is the foundation of the visible Church, and so it is through her as the appointed agent that he becomes our instructor, our spiritual guide, and comforter." And he illustrated his position with six particulars.

Firstly, it is through the Church that Christ offers to convey to us his mercy and grace. "How grateful then should we be for the structure of that visible Church... where we find the blessings we need continuously presented...I do not say that God will not have mercy upon those who never knew the institutions of his Church, but that church is the appointed channel of his grace."

Secondly, the Church of Jesus Christ was founded to instruct his followers in the truths of his Word. The fact of this fallen world is the "humiliating truth," the beginning of that "system of faith to which we look." Fallen man can only be restored to the lost favor of God by remorse, repentance and the "vigorous effort of obedience." The Church is the channel for this restoration, it reminds us of eternal judgment and presents Jesus Christ as the alone meritorious cause of our salvation in all its services and offices. Baptism and the Holy Supper are administered by an authority derived from Christ and none other.

Thirdly, the radical change, the renewal and sanctification of our hearts is "not the work of a day or an hour, and not produced by human agency, and it must be thorough in its effect…" The sanctification required by God must be ongoing, not as a work of irresistible nature, but, while deriving its power and efficacy from the Holy Spirit, must have the constant and unwearied co-operation of the subject himself. "Not that God cannot, if he choose, work irresistibly, but because he deals with us as accountable and rational beings; and while he dispenses the gift of the spirit and gives us a good will to serve him, we are also to work for ourselves."

Fourthly, the Church is the mode through which the Lord can hear and answer our prayers. While God does surely hear the prayers and regard the tears of any who look to him, yet in the services of the sanctuary we are furnished with the form of sound words on which to shape the prayer of our hearts.

Fifthly, the Church strengthens and enlivens us in the pursuit of that eternal life in which we shall join the saints. In baptism we swear to fight on under the banner of Christ and at the holy table we are raised to the anxious and vigorous pursuit of that high calling in Christ which marked the prophets, apostles, martyrs and holy ones of the past.

Sixthly, the Church gives us spiritual support and comfort during this earthly pilgrimage. When we need strength and comfort in the midst of our earthly woes, a strong hand, a supportive embrace, solace in sorrow, where but in the Church of the Redeemer can we expect to find consolation? "A merciful father may and no doubt will listen to the prayer of the closet, and have pity over him that truly sighs in penitence, however retired and obscure may be the corner in which he falls upon his knees confessing his transgressions – but still it is peculiarly the business of the sanctuary and all its employments to exhibit the laws of the Gospel and the terms on which its blessings are to be expected."

So Rudd made obvious the importance which attaches to a suitable and commodious place for the specific employment of the means of grace.

And now he turned to the immediate subject, the new church building, as he congratulated the congregation. They had worshipped for a year and a half in the courthouse, an inconvenience which had helped them concentrate on essentials. Their restored temple was certainly an object of extensive admiration for its neatness, propriety, and "appropriate decoration." He hoped they would long enjoy it.

> But there is admonition blended with these congratulations, for you will not long enjoy this temple, nor will you profit by any exercises here, unless you use your blessings well and carry into active life the spirit and temper of the Gospel.

> These walls, beautiful as they are, will cry out against you if negligent of the purposes of the Saviour through his Church... The **Mene Tekel** of divine displeasure will be recorded among these chaste decorations, if you come not to these courts with penitent hearts and lively faith, with humbleness of mind, and purity of affection.

Pointing dramatically to the monumental bust of Bishop Hobart which now loomed over his hearers like the accusing statue of the Commandante in Mozart's opera of *Don Juan*, Rudd continued.

> That monument to him who addressed to you his last warning, and which imparts to your Temple an interest and beauty not enjoyed by many others, that monument, bearing as it does the admirable lineaments of one of the greatest and best of men, will perpetually frown upon you if you bring not to this house of prayer the simplicity of devotion which marked his own life — the holiness of purpose which he never failed to cherish — the kindness and love which he so constantly declared to be the fulfillment of the law. [Otherwise]...that monument...will become a monument to your disgrace and sorrow in that day when you and I shall stand with him before the bar of eternal Justice."

With this turn to the thought of a hope of eternal life, Rudd reminded his hearers that while "feebleness and decay are creeping with no mistaken pace over many of our frames,"[1] in days to come many, many, would here be born to the Church in Holy Baptism, partake of the

---

[1] At this point one can imagine that he was looking directly at Dr. Burt.

spiritual nutriment of the holy supper, be truly born of God. He admonished them so to use the church below as to be fitted for the services and joys of that Church Eternal in the heavens.

While thus making use of a vocabulary reminiscent of the revivalism of the hour, the fallen state of man, the unutterable vengeance of God's displeasure, the fearful consideration of eternal judgment, Rudd had taken the occasion to make clear the Anglican conviction that the Christian life is a process of nurture, a life which grows more and more, beginning with the justifying regeneration of Baptism and proceeding in continuing sanctification to the end of the journey. Unlike evangelical revivalism, in which so much depended on the human response to an altar call and the emotions which followed, the guided spiritual progress held forth by the Episcopal Church called for a beginning, an initiation, to be followed by the means of grace, sacraments of growth through the stages of life to its consummation in glory.

These would have been truly noble words to have formed John Rudd's last message to the congregation he had served, more or less willingly, for seven years. But he found himself trapped in a situation at the end of his time in Auburn which paralleled the way his service had begun.

While the parish was seeking a successor, he continued to preach at St. Peter's. When the successor was found, the new arrival was not in robust health. Rudd did not move away from Auburn right away. He was asked at times to fill the pulpit, and an unfortunate antipathy developed between the adherents of the two clergymen.

St. Peter's burned to the ground, February 5, 1832. A church of Gothic architecture, constructed of stone, was built at a cost of $ 10,000. It was consecrated August 8, 1833.

Chapter 2

DEATH, DELAY, AND 'DEPARTURE FOR HIGHER SERVICE'

The Ministries of William Lucas (1833 – 1839),
Charles Hackley (November 1839 – April 1840),
and William Croswell (1840 – 1844)

With the new church completed, John Rudd stayed on in Auburn for a considerable period, although he and his family vacated the rectory for which he had so ardently worked, now made historic by the death of the sainted John Hobart. In August of 1833 the vestry formed a committee to repair and put in order the home the parish had acquired five years earlier. This refurbishing process was to be repeated many times over in the history of that semi-private 'parsonage house.'

At the same time the vestry called as its new rector the Irish-born William Lucas, a graduate of the General Seminary in New York and another pupil of John Henry Hobart. Though Rudd had said that he would continue the services at St. Peter's until a new man arrived, the vestry were anxious, in view of the unsettled religious condition of Auburn, to get a pastor and preacher in place. Lucas accepted, and the thirty-four year old minister was sent seventy-five dollars to defray his moving expenses.

As a gesture to Rudd and his family the vestry designated pew number 60 for the former rector's use "during his pleasure." The rest of the pews were put up to auction on an August Monday.

The pernicious system of 'selling' pews and then annually taxing a levy on them was from the beginning and for years after the only method of funding which vestries and other church councils could conceive, either for the construction of a new church or to provide a predictable source of income for the minister's salary. Inherited from an English parish tradition, the American version allowed payment for these pew subscriptions to be spread out in quarterly installments, which was a method that, while encouraging liberality, also invited delay and default. The issue was complicated by the description of selling "the pews and slips in fee simple & not subject to an annuity."[1] In plain English the pews appeared to be sold and not rented. This arrangement may have seemed useful in the exceptional situation of quickly raising money to construct a church or to rebuild a burned one, but it gave rise to the impression that the pew 'owners' actually owned the pews in their spaces forever, and as they were originally configured within an existing building.[2] The fact that a diagram of the pews thus acquired was filed with the county clerk reinforced the concept that they were permanent property. The agreements to pay for a pew were legal contracts and could be enforced at law. In an economy in which cash was scarce the notes signed for a pew could be sold to a third party. Sometimes a pew not paid for would be repossessed and sold again to

---

[1] Vestry Minutes, June 28, 1832.
[2] St. Peter's would be the subject of a state court decision in later years which eventually settled this impossible conception. The case was later reviewed authoritatively by the Hon. Samuel Blatchford, Justice of the Supreme Court of the United States, a former parishioner of St. Peter's.

another. The capacity in such commerce for open friction between the vestry and individuals was obviously very great.

Major repairs and general church expenses were supported by special 'subscriptions,' promises made by individuals who signed on to a list. Sunday offerings were usually for special purposes, such as domestic or foreign missions, or to support retired clergy and their widows, or for the bishop's discretionary fund, or sometimes for the expenses of the communion elements on Sunday. But selling pews brought in the bulk of the income needed for the predictable costs of operating the church. And chief among those costs was the salary of the minister.

By October of 1833 Mr. Lucas and family had moved into the parsonage, and after his interested observation the list of needed repairs grew substantially. The list tells us much about the progress in domestic arrangements being made at the time. Mrs. Rudd had been preparing meals at an open fireplace until in their last years she got one of the new cooking stoves which attached to the fireplace chimney. The Rudds had had no source of water save a well in the yard and a cistern in the basement. It was now found necessary to repair the "eve gutters and roof," [the means of collection of the cistern water], to "paper the lower rooms," [darkened with smoke from the fireplace], "repair the pantry and remove the dum waiter," [used to bring up filled buckets from the cistern in the cellar], and "procure a patent pump & lead pipe to conduct water to the kitchen, put a pump in the cistern, etc." Mrs. Lucas was to have an indoor kitchen sink with hand-pumped water, and an end to those hazardous trips to the yard or the cellar! That these improvements were made under the stewardship of the parsimonious Hackaliah Burt bears witness to the good relationship between the warden-in-perpetuity and the Irish-born rector.

From Tavern

Mr. Lucas was also on very good terms with the rising politician William Seward, and with Seward's wife Frances. In March of 1837, just ahead of the financial panic which began in May, the cleric arranged with Seward for a mortgaged purchase, at four dollars an acre, of 350 acres of land in Chatauqua County from the Holland Patent Land Company. When by 1839 the property had grown in value Lucas declined an offer of six dollars an acre.[3]

Frances Seward's friendship with the Rudds grew very cold as partisans developed in the parish for the two clergymen and their families.[4] She informed her absent husband that she enjoyed Mr. Lucas's pastoral visits and his conversation:

> Mr. Lucas who is a very good man and a good Christian spent an hour with me Tuesday — we had a long and I believe satisfactory conversation on the subject of religion. He is desirous that I should become a communicant in our Church and says that it is not necessary that the rite of confirmation should be first administered — I expressed to him my unbelief in infant baptism — which he said you had mentioned to him — he said he would not attempt to convince me with his own arguments but would send me some books which I promised to read.

---

[3] William Lucas to WHS, Westfield, Chatauqua Co., March 13, 1837; William Lucas to B.J. Seward, Westfield, Chatauqua Co., May 4, 1839. Seward Papers, University of Rochester.

[4] Her aunt Clarinda and her son Augustus went to church on a Sunday before Christmas. "Clary was very much disappointed because Dr. Rudd preached. Muir left the church." FMS to WHS, December 21, 1835.

> I like Mr. Lucas so much that I am apprehensive that he will not continue long with us. The schism in the Church seems to increase. Dr. Rudd with very little of the Christian spirit persists in preaching. On Christmas day a great proportion of the members left the church because he administered the sacrament.
>
> If Dr. Rudd felt as he should do, he would be content to remain quietly at home notwithstanding he is urged to adopt a contrary course by his adherents. He will undoubtedly disunite the congregation and be the means of Mr. Lucas' leaving us if he continues his present course. In the evening of the same day Mr. Lucas came again in the evening accompanied by Dr. Mason — he is also a favorite and their visit was very agreeable to me."[5]

At the church other improvements continued. A sidewalk was laid in front of the church and to its front door. The heating stoves in the church were ordered to be converted to "stove coal." When that innovation proved expensive the appliances had to be changed back to wood, in but one of many episodes in the continuing problems of stoves and heat. Sunday evening services in the church were initiated, as the ladies of the parish bought a number of oil lamps to light the dark church. The weeks-long labor and fellowship of winding the Christmas evergreens took place at the home of the Bostwick family.[6]

Mr. Lucas' ministry was a six year period of numerical church increase and low church income. As he benefited from Rudd's seven previous years of dependable pastorate, Lucas' baptismal numbers at first soared,

---

[5] FMS to WHS, January 2, 1835.
[6] Deborah Dill Bronson.

FROM TAVERN

23 in 1834, 39 in 1835, 18 in 1836 and 24 in 1837, only to decline sharply in 1838 and 1839. The financial depression which ensued from the Panic of 1837 obviously reduced the birthrate, and Lucas' failing health contributed to the downturn in new members. In this ministry period of almost six years there were thirty-five marriages, and on the one occasion when Bishop Onderdonk returned to Auburn, there were thirty-one to present for confirmation. William Lucas was well-liked, and appears to have been a faithful pastor so far as his physical condition allowed.

However in these same six years the vestry was remarkably and understandably short of money. Debt from the construction of the stone church haunted them for years. In 1835 they sold a strip of sixteen feet from the east side of the parsonage lot for six hundred dollars. They refused to pay John Rudd's bill for the three hundred and thirty dollars owed him for services performed after his resignation. In 1836 they sold off the west side structure known as the "Brick School House Building situate on the church lot" for a hundred and fifty dollars and Rudd's former print shop was no more. Within a year of Lucas' arrival they were in arrears to the new rector for salary. When Dr. Humphrey made an arrangement for a paid organist, the vestry declined to honor it.[7]

The rector's failing salary was augmented by "donations." In early 1837 Frances wrote Henry, "Today Mr. Lucas has a donation party ... what to send?" Later she added, "Well I sent $10 to Mr. Lucas. Pa [Judge Miller] was there, he said there were not many people but they received about $200 – $90 in cash."[8] The following year she reported, "Yesterday Mr. Lucas' donation party came round – the day was unpleasant." She

---
[7] Vestry Minutes, July 3, 1837.
[8] FMS to WHS, March 29, 1837.

sent ten dollars by "Pa". "It was not as generally attended as usual. Miss Miller did not approve of it as she thinks Mr. Lucas' salary sufficient for his comfort."[9]

From 1835 the vestry tinkered with the seating arrangement in the church gallery, to gain more pews to sell, the only way they knew of using their chief asset to raise money. Eventually they created sixteen more slips, or pews. Five vestrymen underwrote the project and were allowed to keep any profits from the first time the slips were sold. When in March of 1838 Lucas proposed that they consider enlarging the church to gain forty more pews to sell, they called for bids from a local builder[10] and seemed to think that the projected cost of two thousand dollars would be a good investment, even as they referred to the "depressed pecuniary condition" of the parish. From Auburn Frances reported to Henry, "You will hear that our banks do not redeem their bills. The next step is an injunction I suppose. What is to be the end of all this?"[11] The Panic of 1837 had settled in.

The additional depressing truth was that William Lucas was not a well man. In 1835 the vestry gave him fifty dollars to take a leave for his health and to cover his cost of procuring a supply minister. In 1836, Mrs. Lucas told Frances Seward that she feared for the future existence of the church.[12] By April 1839 the rector was so ill that the vestry told

---

[9] FMS to WHS, April 20, 1838.
[10] "Selover will do it for $2000, twenty-five feet and two more windows." William Lucas to William Henry Seward, January 28, 1839. Seward Papers.
[11] FMS to WHS, May 13, 1837.
[12] "Mrs. Lucas came round this afternoon. Mrs. Lucas is very much afraid we are all going to desert the little church." FMS to WHS, June 28, 1836.

him to suspend services for a few Sundays.[13] He gave up preaching altogether.[14] On August 24, 1839, they arranged with him to take six months off. Within the week, at the age of forty, he lay dead in the rectory.

Frances relayed the sad news to her husband.

> I have just returned from a visit of condolence to poor Mrs. Lucas — Mr. Lucas is no more — he died yesterday at five o'clock in a fit of apoplexy... Yesterday morning Bishop DeLancey breakfasted with him, he was in better spirits than usual, said he hoped to be able to preach again in a few months — after breakfast a carriage was sent for that he might ride as he was accustomed to do daily." [When the carriage failed to appear, Lucas went up to his room, could not breathe, spoke a few words, and fell senseless on his bed. Bled by the physician, he died at five pm.] "I believe Mr. Lucas was more universally beloved by his congregation than any clergyman we have had."[15]

The vestry resolved to wear for thirty days the badge of mourning, a band of crepe on the left arm. They appropriated one hundred dollars for the Lucas family for proper "mourning apparel." The funeral took place in the church on August 29, 1839.

Mrs. Lucas stayed on in Auburn, worried about her future. Frances Seward was a frequent visitor to Mrs. Lucas, and conveyed the widow's

---

[13] "Mr. Lucas has been very ill...," FMS to WHS, July 25, 1839.
[14] "A strange clergyman preached...poor sermon...from New York." FMS to WHS, August 17, 1839.
[15] FMS to WHS, August 28, 1839.

financial concerns to her husband. That fall she reported that Mrs. Lucas was rather despondent about her prospects and added, "write me about what the agreements were between you and Mr. Lucas about the land in Chatauqua — did he ever pay anything toward the purchase?" Mrs. Lucas thought she had something of value there and said that a number of lawyers had offered to help with any transaction, free of expense.[16] As the widow remained in Auburn for several years, her hope continued for some gain from the land her husband had purchased.[17]

THE NEW DIOCESE AND THE NEW BISHOP

The churchmen of the growing Empire State had for more than four years discussed whether to engage in a precedent-breaking decision to divide the state of New York into two dioceses. A decision was finally reached in late 1837. William Seward was invited to join the committee, meeting on August 21, 1838, to designate the boundary lines of the division of the new diocese.[18]

The Diocese of Western New York held its first convention in Geneva on November 1, 1838. Dr. John Rudd was called to the temporary chairmanship in the absence of a bishop of the new jurisdiction. The convention proceeded to an election.

A heated discussion took place on the part of the few adherents of the Rev. Manton Eastburn, a cleric of somewhat "relaxed" churchmanship. They were opposed to the probable election of the more zealous "high"

---

[16] FMS to WHS, September 20, 1839.

[17] "Pray can you tell me anything about...the land in Chatauqua claimed by Mrs. Lucas?" FMS to WHS, September 6, 1841.

[18] Frances relayed the content of the invitation to Seward from acting chairman, the Rev. P. A. Proal of Trinity Church, Utica.

churchman, William Heathcote DeLancey of Philadelphia, described as "extreme, cold, aristocratic, Tory, anti-republican." Dr. Eastburn was the rector of the Church of the Ascension in New York and later became the Bishop of Massachusetts. Dr. DeLancey, scion of an old Westchester County family, was a protégé of Bishop Hobart's and had served as Bishop White's assistant in the Quaker City. He had the added qualifications of previous experience as Provost and professor at the University of Pennsylvania.[19]

The choice seems to have been between two equally able men. When Delancey was elected by a large majority, the convention had chosen the "Hobartian," the stronger churchman of the two. It was considered a great sacrifice on DeLancey's part that he was willing to leave Philadelphia and serve in Western New York.[20] The place of consecration of the new bishop was designated by the convention as St. Peter's Church, Auburn.

The special convention for the consecration of Bishop DeLancey therefore met in St. Peter's on May 7 and 8, 1839. As the event unfolded, "the throngs in the streets and places of public resort showed that an interesting and solemn scene was anticipated."[21] On that Ascension Day the procession was made up of forty-three clergy, one hundred and three lay representatives from forty-four parishes, and four bishops. The consecrators were Alexander Viets Griswold of the "Eastern Diocese," Henry U. Onderdonk of Pennsylvania, Benjamin T.

---

[19] Hayes, 119-124.

[20] "In truth, it was a tremendous sacrifice for DeLancey to leave… his vast circle of loving friends in Philadelphia… Nothing but his Christian heroism… led him to do it." Comment by the Rev. John Brainard, Hayes, 124.

[21] Hayes, 125.

Onderdonk of New York, and George W. Doane of New Jersey. In his sermon, the bishop of Pennsylvania assured the bishop-elect that he would have the cooperation of a zealous and devoted clergy. He emphasized that the apostolic mantle fell on the new bishop where it had been laid down by the beloved Hobart.[22] When William Heathcote DeLancey "rose from his knees a bishop," a second jewel of distinction had been placed in St. Peter's diadem.

That September of 1839 the vestry of St. Peter's again tackled the problem of selecting a new minister. They made a temporary arrangement with the Rev. W.W. Hickox who had helped out in Lucas' absences.[23] Later they procured periodic assistance from Gordon Winslow, rector of Trinity Church, Elmira. When the impecunious vestry offered Winslow the rectorship at six hundred dollars a year and parsonage, he prudently declined.

After consultation with Bishop DeLancey the vestry located the Rev. Charles W. Hackley of New York City, who accepted their call in mid-November. Mr. Hackley had a very tentative commitment to St. Peter's. He evidently regarded it as sort of a port in a storm. Citing the rigors of winter as his reason, he never moved into the parsonage, but asked the vestry to rent it and give him the extra money. They declined to do so. He thriftily roomed in the hotel "Auburn House." His modest ministerial accomplishments included eighteen baptisms and two marriages. Twenty-eight persons were confirmed by Bishop DeLancey.

---

[22] Hayes, 126.

[23] "The boys have been to church this morning. Fred says a man with a very long face preached a very long sermon." FMS to WHS, September 14, 1839.

FROM TAVERN

By the first of April 1840 Mr. Hackley submitted his resignation "for pecuniary reasons," saying that he was sure the vestry could easily find someone more competent than himself! When his better prospects in New York materialized more slowly than he had hoped he offered to serve (in the milder weather) until the vacancy might be filled.

With this turn of affairs the 1840 Annual Meeting of the parish attempted to deal with their steady problem, pew ownership in fee simple, by asking all the pew holders to surrender their claims to permanent tenure of the pews. The vestry proposed to substitute a system of leases paid for by an annual rent. When the vestry, on Bishop Delancey's advice, called the Rev. William Croswell of Boston in that same year, they faced another of their other problems frankly, stating to Croswell that he ought to come to visit Auburn for a meaningful period before he committed himself, so that he might "settle with knowledge of the parish & people, so that we may count on permanency in the arrangement."

After trips back and forth to Boston, Croswell was finally in place by August of 1840.[24] The usual attention and repairs to the now-to-be-occupied rectory were needed. A new stove was considered to heat the church. Services were continued on Sunday evenings and oil had to be purchased for the church lamps. In the fall of 1842 a proposal was made to add a kitchen to the rear of the parsonage. It was considered again in the spring of 1843, and, together with the addition to the building of a "Sunday School" room, the kitchen was completed before 1843 was over. A chimney was erected in the parsonage attic, evidence that the

---

[24] "Our clergyman Mr. Croswell does not return – he is expected every day." FMS to WHS, July 27, 1840. After Frances did hear Mr. Croswell preach, she reported, "I was pleased with his sermon but he falls short of Mr. Lucas in every respect." FMS to WHS, August 2, 1840.

lower fireplaces were being augmented in rooms up and down with new wood stoves, which were connected to the interior chimney by stove pipe. While the rectory heating arrangements were being improved, the ominous addition of the "Sunday School Room" at the rear of the structure proclaimed the semi-public nature of the 'parsonage house,' a feature which was to plague clergy wives for the rest of the building's existence.

These improvements and additions were possible because the parish's financial condition had finally recovered from the Panic of 1837 and the depression which followed it. At the end of 1841 all debts had been paid off, including those incurred at the time of Lucas' funeral, and the late rector's salary arrears, albeit two years late, were paid to Lucas' widow. The Sunday School room, used for weekday prayers and thus also called "the Chapel," received a stove with stove pipe. The ladies of the parish contributed a hundred dollars and also bought the whale oil for lighting winter services in the church.

By mid-1842 Mrs. Seward was ready for a change of rectors.[25] On a July Monday of that year she reported that she had incautiously gone to church twice the day before, and had made herself ill, because the sermon in the morning was so good she went back again in the afternoon of an oppressively warm Sunday. The preacher was Mr. Cocke of Lyons. "Mr. Cocke is a very eloquent preacher. I would not object to an exchange with the people of Lyons."[26]

---

[25] In June 1842 Frances went to church and reported to her husband that she was all tired out from Croswell's sermon. "Mr. Croswell is very dull company." FMS to WHS, June 5, 1842.

[26] FMS to WHS, July 18, 1842.

From Tavern

It seems that in 1844 after less than four years of ministry in Auburn, Mr. Croswell was ready to leave St. Peter's. Taking a summer vacation in New Haven, he wrote to say he was resigning his "interesting cure" for reasons of health and because "family matters" caused him to be so often absent. He airily informed the vestry, "In so eligible a parish you will find no difficulty" in replacing the rector, and proceeded on to what was often termed 'a field of higher service' as rector of the Church of the Advent in Boston. Accepting his resignation, the vestry borrowed a hundred dollars to bring his salary up to date.

Mr. Croswell averaged nineteen baptisms per year in Auburn, a respectable number. His ministerial acts bore up well for the first two years, with good classes for confirmation in 1841 and 1842, 17 and 14 respectively, but the numbers fell to 5 and 6 in 1843 and 1844. The same pattern is shown in the marriages, 8 in 1841, 4 each in 1842 and 1843, and only 2 in 1844. And quite possibly some of the volume in his first year represented delayed baptisms brought about by Mr. Hackley's hesitant ministry.

Arthur Cleveland Coxe

Excursus III:
Arthur Cleveland Coxe visits St. Peter's Church, 1835

In the spring of 1835 Arthur Cleveland Coxe's family moved to Auburn, where his father was a professor at the [Presbyterian] Auburn Seminary. "Cleve" joined them in June after he completed his first year of study at New York University. Strongly attracted to the liturgy as well as the gothic style and pipe organs of the Episcopal Church, the young student took advantage of his father's absence from Auburn to attend service at St. Peter's. At the outset of the morning he looked across the valley from the site of the seminary and saw the church against the backdrop of Fort Hill.[1]

> Sunday, [June] 23rd. Went to St. Peter's this morning. There is something in the situation of this lovely little sanctuary that is peculiarly beautiful. When viewed at sunset, or early in the morning, from our front windows, its fine gothic turrets, emerging from a clump of locusts of a peculiarly verdant foliage, with its golden-tipped points[2] glistening in the mellow rays of the sun, & standing as it does in fine relief against a lofty hill that rises far above it in the background, it presents a picture which the pencil of no artist could improve. When I rose in the morning I looked from my window, & the lovely object did appear so beautiful in the rays of the rising sun, that just tipped the

---

[1] I am indebted to Cynthia McFarland for this passage from the diary of Bishop Coxe. Ed.

[2] These are the "gold balls" to which Frances Seward took exception.

gilded turrets & bathed the rich locusts in its beams, that I determined to attend church there. Accordingly, when "the sound of the church going bell began to summon to the fane," I wended my way thither with joyous feelings, & I trust a grateful heart.

Who that has seen a sabbath in the country does not know that there is something about it, that seems to distinguish it from other days? The air is stiller; the light seems more soft & mellow; the dew on the grass, in the morning, seems to sparkle with a richer luster; & the very birds seem to utter other notes than those with which they court their young loves, during the days of the week. In fact, Nature seems to join with "the multitude of those that keep holy-day." What heart then but must be thankful, what foot would turn aside to-day, from this house of prayer. Did I believe religion a fable, & Christianity a lie, still for the mere rapture of the feeling would I prefer to keep sacred the day, & to join in the holy service & the chanted prayer.

With such feelings I approached the neat little church, & as I a moment delayed to enter, & observed the succession of families, or persons that constantly were pouring in; here a venerable couple with their gay young daughters, each carrying her prayer-book neatly folded in the clean white kerchief; there a young man with a fair creature whose wreathed bonnet & snowy veil proclaimed her a newly made bride – & there perchance a decrepit old woman, in the neat tho' rusty black that told of her widowhood, just creeping along with her staff in one hand, & her prayer-book in the other; & all these disappearing one after one through the arched doorway, [through] which the solemn organ was pealing within; I was forcibly reminded of many descriptions which I *read* of churches in the villages of England, but of nothing which I had ever before *seen* in *America*.

I did not however tarry long without; the temptation within was too powerful. I therefore entered, & took my seat near the door, not wishing to intrude upon the attention of strangers. The interior was neat & even beautiful. There was, it is true, no "storied window richly dight, casting a dim religious light"[3] – nor did any graven effigies of warlike lords, or cross-legged statues of the crusaders, frown on us from the walls; but all was tasteful though exceedingly plain. The paneling was well painted in imitation of oak; the pulpit deck & rails of the chancel were handsomely, not richly carved & the organ was ornamented in correspondence with the general aspect of things, while the only monument that adorned the walls & reminded the worshipper of his mortality, was a neat cenotaph to the memory of the former diocesan, whose bust stood in a little niche over the marble that related his virtues.

The congregation had no appearance of boorishness or rusticity, but if they had not all the airs of a city audience, they certainly had more of that appearance which "becometh those professing godliness." Among them was many a model of a fine manly appearance, & many a

---

[3] The quotation is an approximation of line 159, *Il Penseroso*, John Milton.

graceful feminine figure, that appeared still more graceful when afterwards in the attitude of prayer. While looking around minutely, though I trust neither curiously or vacantly, the clergyman entered & knelt at the desk.[4] He was a fine-looking man, & behaved with true clerical decorum, while he opened the books, & arranged the service of the day. At length the organ ceased, & as we arose for the clergyman to begin the service, I felt truly ready to join in the solemn acclamation — "The Lord is in his holy temple, let all the earth keep silence before him."

The prayers were read & the lessons, much as they ought to be but it was not till after some time that I perceived by the table "covered with a fair white linen cloth," that I was sufficiently fortunate to have fallen upon a celebration of the Sacrament. This discovery accounted to me for the more than usual solemnity I had observed, & also impressed my own mind with a greater awe. The sermon was very good; indeed I was sorry when it was finished, & when "the grace of our Lord &c" was solemnly invoked upon us, as a gentle hint for us to vacate the church "who were not minded to approach the holy table," I however did not leave the holy place, but changed my seat for a more appropriate one in the gallery, where I beheld the holy sacrament.

The whole was ordered with due solemnity and decorum. Amongst the communicants I observed one that attracted more particularly my attention. She was young & beautiful; her dress was neat, tho' not showy not very rich, but her

---

[4] The Rev. William Lucas.

whole carriage & appearance were so heavenly & becoming, what when she had received the "most comfortable sacrament of the body & blood of our Lord Jesus Christ," and retired from the Church, my mind was led into a train of serious & melancholy meditations.

Who was she? What was she? Was she blest in life, or was her only pleasure, that, which I had just seen her partake of? Was it not probable that I should never see here again? In short, is she not soon destined for the grave, & must the grave-worm riot on that lovely cheek? Alas! Alas! But yet if that is the only dishonour, & if she escapes the gnawings of the worm "which dieth not," is she not rather blessed, & the object of my felicitation, rather than of my pity & condolence?

But the service was now over, & I returned to my dwelling, never however I hope to forget this delightful morning, nor that fair being that involuntarily betrayed me into a train of so salutary reflections.

I was afterwards sorry that I had not partaken of the holy communion with them; but my reason was not that I did not wish to, but because I thought my dear father might object, as he is always opposed to me having anything to do with the "Episcopalians."

In 1850 the church was enlarged by a transept and chancel.

Chapter 3

SAMUEL HANSON COXE, JR., COMES AND GOES

1844 — 1846

In a short month after receiving Mr. Croswell's resignation on September 24, 1844, St. Peter's vestry called the Rev. Samuel Hanson Coxe, Jr., as their new rector. Mr. Coxe was then serving his very first parish in Saratoga.

Samuel Hanson Coxe, Jr., was the second son of Samuel Hanson Cox, a Presbyterian divine who had served on the faculty of the Auburn Theological Seminary from 1834 to 1837. Samuel Jr. and his older brother, Arthur Cleveland Coxe, had opted for clerical service in the Protestant Episcopal Church and both adopted the longer spelling of the family name. Arthur Coxe, born in 1818, had a distinguished career in Hartford, Baltimore, and New York, and was chosen as the bishop of Western New York in 1865.

Samuel, born November 13, 1819, was not twenty-five when he accepted Auburn's call, a recent seminary graduate and a very young man compared to the previous clergy who had served St. Peter's. After leaving Auburn he ministered at Oxford, N.Y., and then for twenty years at Trinity Church, Utica. He was described by one who knew him well as "a calm, quiet man, as different as possible from his impulsive poet-brother, with curious limitations of thought in matters theological and ecclesiastical, but with an infinite fund of humour, and much beloved as a pastor."[1]

Arthur Byron-Curtiss remembered him as "a great fisherman, who wrote two small books on the subject." On an ideal trout day which happened also to be Ascension Day, Coxe once told his Utica sexton to post a notice of "no service," which was reworded into a highly visible sign, "No Services Today. Rector Gone Fishing."[2]

Samuel Coxe's brief time in Auburn was a disaster. He had lived in the village as a teenager and was visiting there in the middle of October 1844 when the offer was extended to him to take over immediately as rector. He accepted the position at once, with the proviso that the rectory would be refurbished. The Rev. Mr. Coxe moved to Auburn in late 1844.

He was married on April 10, 1845, to Eliza Cockburn Conkling[3] and the newlyweds were able to occupy the rectory in early May 1845. Mrs. Coxe was a member of a doubly distinguished family. Her politician brother Roscoe Conkling[4] married Julia Seymour, a younger sister of

---

[1] C. W. Hayes, *The Diocese of Western New York* (Rochester 1905), 211.
[2] Arthur L. Byron-Curtiss, " Reminiscences of the Diocese of Central New York, 1888-1950," unpublished manuscript, May 1950, Archives of Diocese of Central New York, 2.
[3] Eliza Conkling was the daughter of Alfred Conkling (1789-1874) and Eliza Cockburn. Elizabeth Cady Stanton described Eliza as "the tall and stately sister of Roscoe Conkling." *Eighty Years And More: Reminiscences 1815-1897*, Elizabeth Cady Stanton (1898), Chapter IV, "Life at Peterboro."
[4] Roscoe Conkling (1829-1888), Mayor of Utica 1858, Member of Congress 1859-1863, 1865-1867, U.S. Senator 1867-1888. Republican.

politician Horatio Seymour.[5] Her brother F. A. Conkling was married to Mary Seymour, Julia's sister. In July of 1845 Eliza Coxe and Mary Seymour Conkling were baptized in St. Peter's by Samuel Hanson Coxe.[6]

When the young rector encountered the financial realities of married life, especially in the circles to which he was accustomed, he announced to the vestry on September 1, 1845, that the agreed stipend of six hundred dollars and parsonage was not enough to meet his needs and that he would not stay with the parish without an increase. An offended vestry, reluctant to see off another rector so soon, responded that in their present "embarrassed condition" the sum demanded was impracticable but that they would circulate a subscription for more salary. The rector could have whatever extra was subscribed, "and collected." From the point of this hint at Coxe's declining popularity things definitely deteriorated over the winter.

Meeting on April 20, 1846, the vestry asked the rector to excuse himself, and "after the rector retired," elected a committee of three to "confer with the rector on the subject of matters relating to the interests of this parish." Obviously Coxe was in deep trouble. A week later the committee made their report to the vestry and were discharged.

Coxe did not deign to reply directly to the committee's concerns. He did proceed to take his case to others in an effort to assemble some

---

[5] Horatio Seymour (1810-1886), Mayor of Utica 1842-1843, Governor of New York 1853-1854, 1863-1864. Democrat.

[6] July 27, 1845. This must have been a "conditional" baptism, reflecting doubt about the "washings" the two young women had previously received.

support from the congregation, and soon, naturally, the word spread that the vestry was trying to oust him.

By the first of June the vestry had had enough and voted a devastating resolution with a revealing preamble. "Whereas a very general dissatisfaction has been for some time existing in this parish with the ministrations of the Rev. S. H. Cox [sic]… a committee has told him that it was the unanimous opinion of the vestry that the interests of the parish would be promoted by an early severance of the existing condition." Since there had been no reply from Mr. Coxe and he had continued to give publicity to the proceedings, the vestry declared that their relations with him were "dissolved." He was to be paid through August first, and unless other provision could be made for the conduct of services by someone else, the church would be closed!

A week later, the vestry had cooled off a bit. The resolution was reworded, with no mention of closing the church. The attempt to lock the rector out could have stumbled over the reality that as rector he had formal possession of the key. That same day Rector Coxe fired off an angry reply to the original resolution, doubtless calling on his rights, and saying some harsh things he was later advised to retract.

On June 17 the vestry met with Bishop DeLancey. Whether they called the bishop in or whether Coxe had done so is not certain. But the vestry were moved to reconsider matters once more. They referred their relations with Mr. Coxe to "the Bishop of the Diocese for counsel and advice." The bishop advised all of them to give up their angry exchanges and for Mr. Coxe to resign voluntarily by the first of September. Coxe then withdrew his June 8 letter to the vestry and the original was returned to him. The vestry minutes stood as recorded, but the "dissolution" resolution was now also formally withdrawn.

But Coxe wouldn't leave the matter or the record in the vestry's hands. Sometime prior to September 1, 1846, he borrowed the Vestry Minute Book from the business office of the trusting clerk of the vestry, J. H. Bostwick. He dampened and erased half a page of the ink record, pasting over it a new half page. Just before he left Auburn for his next post in Oxford he returned the book to Bostwick's office.

The vestry were furious when they viewed the altered and faded pages of their violated Record Book, and learned from a contrite Bostwick that he had allowed the departing rector to take the book in good faith and trusted him to return it unharmed. The vestry was partly composed of lawyers to whom records were sacred, and though the entire group was glad to see the last of the unbowed Coxe, they formally entered into their desecrated minute book a new resolution, roundly condemning one who would commit such an "act of mutilation."[7]

Samuel Hanson Coxe's brief tenure in Auburn can be understood as the conflict brought on by a stubborn young man of good family and high connections who insisted on his own way of doing things in a village he had known as a boy. It is patently evident that he failed to please. The parish expected something which he would not or could not supply. He collided with the vestry by demanding something from them which they would not or could not produce. When the relationship between them had soured completely the vestry mistakenly thought they could discharge him for that reason alone.

Bishop DeLancey advised them all to back down, but he saw the reality that Mr. Coxe's ability to minister effectively in Auburn was finished. So the bishop persuaded Coxe to resign and the uncertain problem

---

[7] Vestry Minutes, October 6, 1846.

raised by a vestry attempting unilaterally to dissolve pastoral relations was avoided. Coxe, together with his pregnant wife,[8] moved to the parish in Oxford rather quickly and seemed not to have suffered permanently from the impasse at St. Peter's.[9]

In 1870, soon after Eliza Conkling Coxe had passed away, when the Rev. Mr. Coxe received one of Dr. Brainard's printed invitations to come to the consecration of the new St. Peter's church, he sent back a melancholy reply. Though he had several times returned to St. Peter's for service in 1851 and 1852, he solemnly declined, in his present period of mourning, to join in a celebration.

> I must decline, dear brother, to attend. The occasion is eminently festive; while for me, a visit to St. Peter's would inevitably be fraught with a predominance of sad and sorrowing associations. My sympathies would be more with deceased Rectors, and deceased wife, than with the living parish.

---

[8] Their son, Alfred Conkling Coxe, was born in May of 1847.
[9] Coxe's record in Auburn shows 6 marriages, 11 confirmed in a single class, with 12 baptisms in 1845 and 14 in 1846.

"Grace, <u>grace</u> unto it," rather than ——— "shoutings."[10]

With sincere congratulations however, and wishing you felicity, I remain,

Affectionately yours,
S. Hanson Coxe.[11]

Samuel Hanson Coxe, Jr.

---

[10] This expression, placed in quotes by Coxe, seems to be a commonplace, used against the "shoutings," the ecstatic expressions of the "big meetings." The phrase was used against revivals in a variant form by Orestes Brownson in his Auburn Universalist period, where Brownson describes an opponent as confident that "when the celestial beings bring forth the headstone and some are crying grace, grace, unto it, others will cry, fire, fire…" Brownson said this would be reminiscent of a Methodist Camp Meeting scene. *The Early Works of Orestes A. Brownson, Vol. I, The Universalist Years 1826-29*. Patrick W. Carey, ed. (Milwaukee, 2000), 30.

[11] Brainard's bound book of replies and mementos.

Reverend Walter Ayrault

Chapter 4

Pastoral Progress:
The Ministry of the Rev. Walter Ayrault, 1847 — 1852

After the impasse with the Rev. Samuel Coxe the vestry of St. Peter's soon made a number of offers to clergy, but found no one who would accept. Perhaps the troubles with Coxe had made candidates wary of St. Peter's, a parish with a vestry that had dared to attempt to discharge the rector.

In late July 1846 they began a series of calls to several priests, starting with Charles H. Platt of Rochester, with the request that he come immediately. To have the position covered quickly might reduce any criticism of the vestry from those parishioners who possibly favored Coxe. On October 6 they offered the work to William E. Eigenbrodt. Three weeks later they called John H. Fish. When he declined they tried Eigenbrodt again, but by March 1847 no one had accepted.

At this point in 1847 the subdued vestry finally consulted directly with Bishop DeLancey, asking him for the temporary services of the Rev. Mr. Walter Ayrault, a recently ordained deacon. Ayrault promptly came to Auburn and it was soon evident that there was a very good match. In April 1847 the vestry asked him to stay on and become rector after he was ordained a priest.[1]

---

[1] The Rev. Walter Ayrault was born in Geneva November 28, 1822 and died there October 19, 1882.

From Tavern

Walter Ayrault began services at St. Peter's on the Third Sunday in Lent, March 7, 1847. From that day the young man of twenty-three kept a complete record of his ministerial acts, carefully writing them down in a small ledger. In 1953 the thin notebook happily was returned to the parish by an antique dealer and forms the basis of much of our knowledge of him and his time of service.

It is apparent that the young deacon went to work in an energetic fashion. Enthusiastic, with the dark hair of youth, the bachelor from Geneseo put new life into St. Peter's. A protégé of Bishop William H. DeLancey, he was filled with the zeal of the Oxford Revival of "church spirit" which he combined with a high degree of fraternal relationship with his fellow clergy of Western New York. He was, as his contemporary Charles Hayes reported, "another of those noble and large-hearted men for whom Bishop DeLancey's leadership seemed to have a special charm."[2]

In great contrast to the parish's rather forlorn experience with Mr. Coxe, Walter Ayrault's time at Auburn was a story of progress. His whole ministry, said Hayes, "was brightened with the fervour of the earliest and best years of the 'Oxford Movement,' and he kindled it in all who came in contact with him; bringing lofty ideals into the commonest things of life by his charm of person and conversation."[3] Small wonder that Ayrault's longest service, after several parishes, was as chaplain at Hobart College.

His "strong church" zeal manifested itself in a consistent refusal to recognize the validity of the Universalist Church, which was at that time

---

[2] Hayes, 212.
[3] *Ibid.*, 212.

fairly vigorous in Auburn. The Rev. William L.H. Mellen, pastor of that society, invited Ayrault on one occasion to join in some activity for the support of the "The Cayuga Asylum for Destitute Children." Ayrault refused, saying "I could never associate myself with you in any interprise in which you act or appear as a <u>teacher of Christianity</u> in the community...regarding as I do the peculiar religious principles and the whole system of Universalism with <u>the utmost abhorrence</u>... as teaching for truth what I consider to be <u>utterly false</u>."[4] This youthful fervour was to put a shadow on his relationship with his most prominent family, the Miller and Sewards.

Every page of Ayrault's assiduous record book reflects his zeal and success, his concern for his own flock. Paid fifty dollars a month, he delighted in the observance of the full weekly and daily calendar of the Church, the saints' days and the ember weeks in which he and the other young deacons of the diocese met in Oswego or Syracuse for several days of prayer and conference about the ministry they had just begun. Until he was ordained a priest he exchanged pulpits on the communion Sundays with older men in the area who could officiate at the sacrament. After he was made a priest he consistently provided the same service for his younger colleagues. His record book is replete with the names of area clergy or Geneva faculty as they exchanged back and forth in a process which makes clear the high degree of clergy collegiality of the period.[5]

---

[4] Walter Ayrault to William L.H. Mellen, Auburn, New York, November 10, 1852. Seward Papers.

[5] A large factor in the exchanges was the development of the railroad connections between Auburn and Syracuse (after 1834), and between Auburn and Rochester, via Geneva and Canandaigua (after 1840). In 1841 one could travel from Albany to Buffalo, via nine different railroad companies. Only after 1853 was there a direct line from Syracuse to

From Tavern

Auburn, conveniently located and with a fine church, was frequently chosen by Bishop DeLancey as the place for pre-ordination examinations and diocesan conventions. Ayrault's own class of advancement was ordained priest there in August 1847. Before that he had signed the register as "Deacon and Rector-elect."

At that point he acquired an assistant. A newly married school teacher and candidate for ordination, George C. Foote, was designated as "Assistant Minister." Foote taught a Parish School in the rooms at the rear of the rectory. Since the unmarried Ayrault lived elsewhere, the "parsonage house" living quarters were rented to A. Suydam for a hundred and fifty dollars a year.[6] Foote and Ayrault jointly conducted three services on Sundays and read weekday prayers in the church. Bachelor Ayrault, who traveled about a good deal to Geneseo, Rochester, and New York City,[7] could count on married Mr. Foote to look after things. Ordained deacon in early 1848, Foote gave up the leadership of the school in March 1849 and moved away from Auburn the following November.

The congregation prospered under Ayrault's attention.[8] In 1847 it consisted of about seventy-five families and "over 100" communicants, with sixty-six Sunday School scholars and fifteen teachers. A year later the parish had grown to one hundred and eleven families, one hundred

---

Rochester, reducing Auburn to a secondary route.

[6] Ayrault's sister Mary came to live with him in 1850.

[7] Frances Seward went to church on Thanksgiving in 1847, "to hear Mr. Foot read a sermon — Mr. Ayrault is still with his father." FMS to WHS, November 27, 1847.

[8] Baptisms were numerous; 26 in 1847, 46 in 1848, 46 in 1849, 36 in 1850, 26 in 1851, and 26 in the half of 1852 for which Ayrault was responsible. Overall he presented 86 people for confirmation.

and fifty-six communicants, and a Sunday School of eighty pupils and eighteen teachers. In 1850 the "Parish School" numbered sixty scholars, who went on a "Pic Nic" to Fort Hill with the Sunday School for an August supper outing.[9] Miss Adeline Holland now rented the school rooms, where she was assisted by Miss Maria Hiser.[10]

After Ayrault became a priest in 1847 one hundred and twenty-five copies of a booklet, "Familiar Instruction for Public Worship," were distributed in the pews of the church. At his first Christmas in 1847 he noted that the church was decorated "simply with trees and boughs of evergreen, and a large cross of greens marked I.H.S. was at the back of the chancel." The use of the unadorned Christmas Tree is evidence of Ayrault's fondness for "high church" English ways.[11]

In November 1848, the faithful pastor, newly instituted as rector, started a Bible class on Tuesday evenings at six thirty. In 1851 he used the same weekly period for a class on "Evidences of Natural and Revealed Religion."

Both the Sunday School children and the Ladies Guild began to work on projects and money raising. On Saturday afternoons in 1847 and following years, in the months before Christmas, the children labored to make "useful and fancy items," with sales of $137.44 in 1849. [As a comparison, the plate offering on Easter in 1848 worked out to a scant

---

[9] Before it became a cemetery Fort Hill was a park and gathering place. "Howe delivered his [Fourth of July] oration on Fort Hill." FMS to WHS, July 7, 1842.
[10] Miss Maria C. Hiser was General John Chedell's niece. She lived at 17 James Street and was a sponsor/witness at a total of nine baptisms, beginning in 1853.
[11] If a deceased person was English, Ayrault noted it in parenthesis.

From Tavern

nine cents per communicant!] With the first year's proceeds the 'children' bought a font for sixty dollars. The ladies held their sale on Easter Tuesdays, raising a hundred and eleven dollars in 1851, of which one hundred went to "Minnesota Missions, St. Paul."

The uncertainties of life and death appear clearly in Ayrault's record book. Frequently to the notation of a private communion or baptism in the home would be added a parenthetical "(dead)" followed by notice of the burial of the same adult or child. On August 3, 1849 the parish observed the state and national Fast Day proclaimed on account of the widespread ravages of cholera. But the worst scourge for Auburn, an outbreak of scarlet fever, was in 1848 from March to late summer. Ayrault noted that it was "now very prevalent, especially among children." There were eight deaths from scarlet fever in the parish, and a number of baptisms were performed, obviously for fear of the deadly disease.

The Rev. Elishah W. Hager, a recently ordained priest, was appointed Chaplain to the Auburn State Prison in January 1851 and began his duties on February first.[12] From then on whenever Bishop DeLancey made a formal visitation to St. Peter's he began the day at the prison chapel at the nine o'clock Sunday Morning Prayer and Sermon which Hager conducted for the prisoners. Sing Sing's new chaplain, the Rev. M. M. Wells, came in March 1851 to join the Auburn clergy for the Bishop's Visitation. It seems that both chaplaincies, paid for by the state, began as Episcopalian fiefdoms.

In E. W. Hager, who remained in Auburn until 1852, Ayrault once more had a fellow cleric to share the local services and ministrations.

---

[12] Hager was married.

The rector filled in at the prison when the chaplain wanted to be away and Hager helped with the growing needs of St. Peter's which were a testimony to Ayrault's productive work.

Two years of Walter Ayrault's ministry resulted in obvious expansion. The annual Parish Meeting in April 1849 was followed by several months of deliberation about enlarging the church to meet the need for more space and more pews to rent. In late summer 1849 a decision was reached. A deeply recessed window would be added to enlarge each side of the church, creating transepts in the east and west walls. A furnace would be placed in the basement, eliminating the space taken up by the troublesome stoves.[13] The chancel, no longer to be a mere platform, would be recessed as a sacred alcove eight feet in depth and a vestry [robing] room constructed behind it.[14] All this was estimated to cost twenty-five hundred dollars. It would gain forty pews. At the same time the "Sunday School rooms" at the rear of the parsonage would receive a second story to accommodate the growing classes.

Amid some legal controversy[15] the work of enlarging St. Peter's Church was started in late August 1849. At the end of September the rear north wall was taken down and services thereafter were held in the Court

---

[13] Vestry Minutes, July 24 and August 4, 1849.

[14] That the vestry room was centered we know from the decision in 1853 to establish "a black walnut chancel rail, with gate opposite the Vestry Room door," Vestry Minutes, February 23, 1853.

[15] "Bronson makes himself ridiculous by suing the vestry to prevent enlargement because his pew would be further removed from the pulpit. He argued his own case — Goodwin that of the vestry. Goodwins personal abuse of Bronson gained B. some sympathy." FMS to WHS, September 24, 1849. [This was Parliament Bronson, Esq., husband of Deborah Dill.]

House.¹⁶ On return to the church in mid March 1850, the vestry thanked Sheriff Swift for the use of the county court house. In March Bishop DeLancey made a Visitation to confirm, and to see the enlarged church. The expanded St. Peter's proved more and more useful for episcopal acts.¹⁷ In the rains of May [May 27, 1850] the Rev. Mr. Ayrault planted ivy at the walls of the church, noting:

> on this day I planted a <u>slip of English Ivy</u> from <u>Lambeth Palace</u> <u>Canterbury</u> [sic], England in front of the Church, on <u>East Side of Tower</u>, under window; also <u>a slip of Scotch Ivy</u> from <u>Dryburg</u> [sic] <u>Abbey</u>, Scotland, against <u>South side of West Transept</u>: also an <u>American Ivy</u> in S. West angle of Tower: (These vines given by Mrs. Alvah Worden¹⁸ of Canandaigua) — many vines and trees planted about the church this year.

Regardless of the foundation plantings more extensive repairs and repainting were resumed in August 1850 and the congregation once more made do with the Court House for Sundays. General Abraham Gridley, a distinguished member, died in November and his funeral could not take place from the church. Services were cancelled from late November until after Christmas. The Court House was occupied for

---

¹⁶ "Our church is all torn to pieces, as is the Presbyterian." FMS to WHS, September 24, 1849.

¹⁷ On a rainy Sunday Frances reported "Augustus and Fred have gone to church… The Bishop is here and two or three young clergymen are to be ordained." FMS to WHS, May 26, 1850. [The four ordained priest that day were Noble Palmer, Malcolm Douglass, E.W. Hager and G.H. McKnight. Ayrault Journal.]

¹⁸ Mrs. Worden was the former Lizette Miller, she of the dark, chestnut curls.

the time with an exhibition of paintings. Ayrault was called away just before Christmas by the death of his father. On Christmas Day services were crammed into "Mrs. Rosamund Orton's rooms — South Street."[19]

By January 5th, 1851 the congregation was back in occupancy of the remodeled church, with no apparent loss in strength or number. All was in order when Bishop DeLancey made his annual visitation in late March and Ayrault noted that "the Bishop examined the youth…in the catechism, at the chancel. Visited the Parish-School building & grounds." The effect of the alterations had been to create a church eighty-six feet long, fifty-eight feet wide at the transepts, forty-two feet wide in the nave, with one hundred and twelve pews down and twenty-five in the gallery, a total accommodation for over five hundred people.

A happy feature of the parish in Mr. Ayrault's time was the addition of Clarence A. Seward and his bride, Caroline DeZeng, the foster daughter of Bishop DeLancey. In June of 1847 Clarence, himself the ward of his uncle William Henry, had determined to be baptized and confirmed. Frances informed her husband that "Clarence writes me that he is desirous of being baptized and also asks permission to come home at the time of the Bishop's next visit some time next month to be confirmed. The influence of the Bishop's daughter has not failed to operate on his susceptible mind. I hope it may lead to goodness."[20] In August 1850 Frances, taking the train, visited the DeLanceys in Geneva. "Went as far as Geneva with Clarence to see the DeLancey family. Caroline is very pretty and pleasing in her manners — my conversation was chiefly with

---

[19] Mrs. Gerrit V. Orton, General John Chedell's sister-in-law, obviously possessed a spacious home. She moved to Brooklyn in 1857. Her husband died November 18, 1846.

[20] FMS to WHS, June 14, 1847. Clarence was confirmed at St. Peter's on July 9, 1847.

the father and mother. Him you know — Mrs. DeLancey is a well-favored pleasing person." The young couple were married in Geneva at Eastertime in 1851, and moved to Auburn where Clarence was a member of the firm. Naturally they attended church.[21] And they made an additional Seward presence in the social life of Auburn. "The gay portion of the society here are amusing themselves with masquerades. I am told that Mrs. Clarence Seward gives one tonight. There have been two at Blatchford's ... Is not this a grand city?"[22]

The expanded church was filled when the father-in-law of William H. Seward, Judge Elijah Miller, passed away in November of 1851. It was rumoured in the village that Mr. Ayrault had elected to consult the bishop about the propriety of conducting the funeral in the Episcopal church. Judge Miller, who had always kept a pew in St. Peter's, also maintained one in the Universalist Church, of which Frances Seward herself, equally broad in her views, occasionally made use.[23] Ayrault, as previously noted, would have nothing to do officially with the Universalists, even when they combined with the Presbyterians and Methodists for a public service in observance of the sudden death of President Zachary Taylor.[24]

---

[21] "Fanny and I have been to church alone. We found Clarence and Carnie there." FMS to WHS, June 15, 1851.

[22] FMS to WHS, September 8, 1851.

[23] Prevented by a rain in 1847 from going to St. Peter's, Frances thought she would take an umbrella and walk to the Universalist Church, "where Grandpa has a foot bench put in his pew." FMS to WHS, September 14, 1847. In mid-1852 she went on Sunday to the Universalist church to hear Mr. Mullen discourse on the death of Hosea Ballou. FMS to WHS, June 28, 1852.

[24] "Mr. Ayrault spoke truly and touchingly of General Taylor's death." [But did not participate with Universalist Mr. Austin, two Presbyterians and one Methodist in public service.] Noting that there had been

Mr. Ayrault's strong church attitude in these matters wore painfully, if not irritatingly, on Frances Seward. And she informed her husband, "As much as I love our church I fear sometimes they will drive me away from it. It seems to have been the town talk this winter that Mr. Ayrault would not venture to have the remains of our honored father taken into the church until he had consulted the Bishop. – After all he has done for the church." She testily asserted that she would wait for an explanation from Mr. Ayrault.[25]

The strong church views of Ayrault and his bishop continued to weigh on Frances Seward. In early June of 1852, after going to church with the children, she expressed her mixed feelings about St. Peter's and some of its clergy. "There are so many tender recollections associated with our Church that I never enter it after a long absence without a feeling of sadness. There is so much in her liturgy attractive and soothing that I lament more and more the narrow bigotry and intolerant spirit of her clergy, but like all other things of mortal mould she has a mixture of good and ill."[26]

At two pm on Sunday, November 16, 1851, Judge Miller's funeral was conducted in the church and interment took place in the brand new Fort Hill Cemetery, the "first interment" there. When Thanksgiving Day arrived, Bishop DeLancey, perhaps trying to shore up Mr. Ayrault's popularity, honored St. Peter's by preaching at the ten thirty service, where, in a variation of the custom of a "Donation Day" for the

---

four or five deaths from cholera, Frances added that she told the children not to eat any cherries, [a surfeit of which on the Fourth of July, washed down with cold milk, had been the cause of President Taylor's death.] FMS to WHS, July 14, 1850.

[25] FMS to WHS, May 28, 1852.
[26] FMS to WHS, June 6, 1852.

minister, he invited the congregation "to meet the rector sociably in the evening" at Mr. Ayrault's residence. "A very pleasant re-union — calculated to do good," noted Ayrault in his journal.

A week later a properly hesitant Mr. Ayrault called at the Sewards, to solicit a pledge to increase the endowment of the bishop's salary.[27] Not venturing to bring his request to Frances alone, he sent a letter with the pledge form directly to Seward.[28]

For Christmas 1851 the proud rector highlighted his new altar and pulpit by concentrating all the decorative evergreens in the chancel. Apparently he took it upon himself to reverse the lectern and pulpit from one side to the other, and there was some protest later on the part of those who thought they had paid for a pew in front of the pulpit, only to find themselves staring at the lectern.

In the following March, 1852, he wrote in his journal that he had been officiating at St. Peter's for five years. "Hitherto hath the Lord helped us," he noted from I Samuel 7:12, his anniversary text, and added, "*Gratias Tibi Domine!*"

Bishop DeLancey made an annual visitation to the parish in March of 1852, confirming one man and twelve young women, among them four Sarahs and three Marias. DeLancey had recently accepted appointment by the House of Bishops to represent the American Church at the

---

[27] "Mr. Ayrault was here last night and intimated that he came to ask a donation for the increase of the Bishop's salary, but did not say so directly, saying he should call again. What shall I tell him?" FMS to WHS, December 4, 1851.

[28] Walter Ayrault to William H. Seward, December 19, 1851, Seward Papers.

closing ceremonies of the three hundredth anniversary of the founding of the "Venerable Society for the Propagation of the Gospel," the famous "S.P.G." which had played a decided role in building up the Church of England in the American colonies. The bishop asked the energetic young rector, an accomplished Anglophile, to accompany him on an extended trip to England. When the bishop sailed for London on May 29, 1852, Walter Ayrault was with him to serve as Bishop's Chaplain for the formal tour. Together they traveled around England for four months, sight-seeing, attending grand jubilee services, and enjoying the peculiar celebrity of "an American Bishop," an absolute rarity in England.

Upon his return from the glories of the tour Ayrault handed in his resignation as rector of St. Peter's as of the end of 1852. The vestry tendered him a heartfelt testimonial. "In parting with you we desire to express our deep conviction of your devoted piety and zeal, an admiration of your faithful and untiring labors, our love for your pure and unspotted character, and our ardent wishes for your future welfare."[29]

He had made no entries in his journal after mid-May, and with DeLancey's blessing, he moved on to minister in Canandaigua.

---

[29] Vestry Minutes, October 11, 1852.

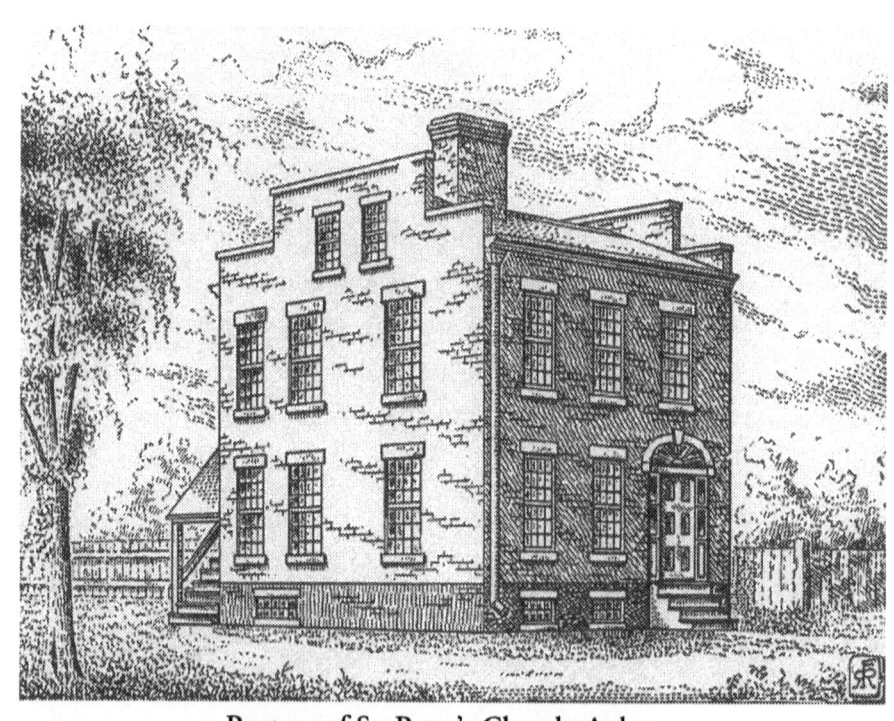

Rectory of St. Peter's Church, Auburn
Where Bishop Hobart died, 1830.

Excursus IV:
People of Color

People of color were members of St. Peter's from the beginning. The earliest ones were servants belonging to the Bostwick and Cumpston families. And, according to Azuba Terry, from early days Judge Miller had a very popular "negro servant named Pete" who called the dances and passed the refreshments at balls and gatherings for young and old. There is no evidence that talented Peter Crosby was present at services, but it seems possible that he was there to attend to the Judge's wants.

Over the first half century of the church's existence the parish register occasionally took notice when people of color were baptized, confirmed, and buried. The following list gives the notations. From the outset a person of color was in the communicant list. After 1858 no notice of color was written in the records.

Of interest is the change in style of notation. At first black people were listed by their familiar "first" names. Eventually last names and social titles were recorded.

In January of 1817, a primary communicant list of just thirty members compiled by Mr. McDonald included Jenny, "black servant to Mrs. Cumpston."

From Tavern

On March 8, 1820, Charlotte, "a colored person belonging to Mrs. Jonathan Booth of Skaneateles," was confirmed, as was an otherwise unidentified "Betsy (colored.)" Charlotte was placed on the communicant list in April 1820.

July 23, 1826, "Jemima, a black woman aged 28 years," was buried, in the public ground.

In November 1827, "Sally Rose (black)" was listed as a communicant,

March 4, 1829, the death of "Flora, about 16, of consumption, a black woman belonging to the family of G. B. Throop, Esq." was entered. Flora was the child of Sybil and Eleven, servants of the Bostwicks.

March 25, 1829, David Wimmer was married to Sally Rose "(blacks.)"

August 10,1831, Mr. Baker of the Methodist church buried a black woman. "In Mr. Rudd's absence."

December 4, 1831, "baptized on her death bed, Sybil (a black), formerly belonging to the Bostwick family." She was entered as a communicant on December 16, and buried December 22, noted as "Sybil, a black woman." [Sybil and Eleven , her husband, were also the parents of George, who, according to Deborah Dill, lived with (Baptist) Nathaniel Garrow.]

May 15, 1842, "Miss Sarah Dean Jackson (colored)"was confirmed.

January 1, 1843, "Grace a colored child in the service of Capt. Wm. Swain," was baptized.

November 1, 1844, the list of Sunday School children included, "Patty (colored.)"

March 19, 1848, "Charles Duffin (a colored man)" was confirmed.

In 1850, "Mrs. Mary Anna Burns (colored woman)" was added to the communicant list. She remained on the list through 1865.

December 4, 1858, "Fannie M. Freeman (colored)," was buried in North Street Cemetery.

And in Walter Ayrault's Journal there is this entry: "May 19, 1848. On Wednesday P.M. Rev. Wm. C. Munroe (deacon), a colored man, was present. He resides in Detroit and is now here on a mission collecting funds to finish a church for his people there. He brings a letter of commendation from his bishop. We raised for him about $25.00."

Chapter 5

Ministries of E. H. Cressey, C. H. Platt, J. W. Pierson: 1852 – 1863

The Civil War Begins

While Walter Ayrault was absent on his English tour, the Sunday services had been regularly[1] supplied by the Rev. E.W. Hager, the prison chaplain.[2] After Ayrault's resignation various clergymen were employed to supply St. Peter's for brief periods. The duties were taken at times by E.W. Hager; George Foot; Daniel W. Warren (a new prison chaplain who arrived in August 1852); and Benjamin Hale of the Hobart faculty.

When the enlarged church had been completed, Mr. Ayrault had apparently arranged the chancel furnishings to suit himself, shifting the pulpit from one side of the chancel to the other. Those who had paid for the pew directly in front of the pulpit in its former position now demanded that it be restored! The Vestry agreed and complied.[3]

---

[1] "We have no settled preacher in our church while Mr. Ayrault is absent, but the Church is always opened." FMS to WHS, June 28, 1852.

[2] Frances Seward heard Mr. Hager on the doctrine of the Trinity. "He was wiser than some divines who preach on the same subject as he commenced by saying it was entirely beyond human comprehension." FMS to WHS, June 13, 1852.

[3] Vestry Minutes, January 10, 1853.

From Tavern

A degree of prosperity seems to have affected Auburn at the time of the general growth of the national economy during the Mexican war and as the effects of the Gold Rush of 1849 spread over New York. In January of 1853 the Vestry decided to create a new altar rail and to install gas light in the church. At the same time they raised the promised annual salary at which they would call a new rector from six hundred dollars to one thousand dollars. Bishop DeLancey's recommendation for the post was the Rev. Ebenezer Harrison Cressey, then in Tennessee. Mr. Cressey, ordained deacon in 1838, had been rector of Lockport, New York, from 1841 to 1845, and had founded a school for girls there in that period.

The cautious vestry, seeking to engage a rector who would be sufficiently satisfied with St. Peter's to stay a while, sought to know why a clergyman from Western New York had wandered off to Tennessee after only a little more than four years in Lockport. They wrote for references from laymen who were knowledgeable and were eventually assured that Cressey had been urged to stay on in Lockport, but that he was young and zealous and ambitious and wished to better himself.

At the time of the call to Auburn in 1853 Mr. Cressey was over forty years old. He and his wife Emma had a family which included two grown children, Frances and Charles, who were of sufficient age to be witnesses at impromptu weddings in the Auburn rectory. His mother, Amanda, also lived with them. Because the parsonage had been rented during bachelor Ayrault's years, it was necessary to put the house in good repair and to reclaim one of the rear 'school rooms' for family use. From February 23 to April 18, 1853, these adjustments were gradually accomplished.

Financial things did not proceed smoothly. In a year's time pew rents were seriously in arrears and more pews had to be squeezed in by realignment of the rows. The heating in the church was unsatisfactory and a larger furnace was installed. In July of 1855 Cressey was ill and consideration was given to an assistant for him. Caught in an economic downturn the church was $800 in debt in November of 1855 but out of debt by March of 1856, only to suffer the expense of more repairs on the parsonage a month later.

In August 1856 Cressey made the demand that he needed more support for his family, and threatened to resign if his salary were not increased to $1500! The vestry said that they would try to find an additional $300 [over the contracted $1000]. But the vestrymen, shying from the problem, and likely suspecting that Mr. Cressey suffered from endemic economic dissatisfaction, avoided the responsibility of their meetings all that fall. There was no quorum at vestry sessions until November, when an exasperated Cressey presented an urgent memorial saying that the vestry must make a plan to raise more money. But no plan developed.

In December of 1856 Mr. Cressey asked Governor William Seward to commend him for appointment to the Board of Visitors of West Point. The following January Cressey renewed his efforts to supplement his income by such an appointment.[4]

Meanwhile the Panic of 1857 struck. The end of the Crimean War had reduced the European demand for American wheat as Russian wheat once more came to market. Overheated investment in American railroad development began to collapse. The great American boom of

---

[4] E.H. Cressey to William H. Seward, Albany, December 15, 1856, January 6, 1857, Seward Papers.

the 1850s was over, and the banking system of the increasingly disunited United States failed from August 1857 onward. The price of gold sank due to overproduction and in a symbolic moment the gold ship " S.S. Central America" foundered off the east coast in a September 1857 hurricane.

In April 1857, with the rector absent from the meeting, the vestry resolved to raise more money. Again, nothing specific was done.

In April of 1858 a memorial was presented to the vestry from "numerous members of the congregation," who were spurred on no doubt by the continuing demands of rector Cressey. The appeal to the vestry stressed the importance of devising better means to defray expenses, but seems to have received no reply from them. A new furnace had to be purchased for the rectory and the cistern was repaired. The vestry chose to tinker with the matter of the ownership of the pews, either to 'revalue' them at a higher price or to try to get the 'owners' to surrender their titles to the vestry who would then rent them back to the former occupants. A. H. Burt, son of the formidable Hackaliah, reported that it was always his father's idea that the pews should belong to the vestry.

However all this was of little use to a self-described "overworked" Cressey. In May of 1858, informing the vestry that he had been "enfeebled" by Lent, he was granted a leave of absence for his health. His urgent necessities were waiting on his unpaid salary, and the vestry response was to plan a Thanksgiving 'donation,' a gathering of gifts for the parsonage family.[5] Cressey's hope for more personal income met

---

[5] Mr. Cressey was a worker. Over the six years he baptized 202, presented 82 for confirmation, and officiated at 71 weddings, many at the

competition in the solicitation of the Missionary Bishop of Shanghai, the Rt. Rev. William J. Boone, who visited St. Peter's that year on the Sunday after Christmas.

The financial practice of the church in those days, a time of delayed debts and promissory notes, required the clergyman to carry many of the parish's obligations, to pay most of the day to day minor costs incurred, and to receive reimbursement, sometimes with interest, much later. Salaries were often treated the same way, as a debt the parish owed and would pay when it could, sometimes with interest. Pew rents were paid with promissory notes, at interest, the actual payment of which could be put off until convenient for the debtor.

As 1859 began the vestry had not retrieved title to all the pews. But by April they managed to pay the rector in full for the previous year of 1858, and to advance him the partial payment of $101.92 on the current year. Over the summer the vestry again did nothing about fiscal problems and failed to obtain a quorum in September.[6]

Thus it was that on October 24, 1859, Cressey, with a very short letter, resigned with two weeks notice. The vestry, summoned to meet five days after receiving this letter, initially failed of a quorum. Eventually they managed to meet and to write the departing rector that they deeply regretted the circumstances which had induced him to sever the

---

parsonage and some as late as nine in the evening!

[6] Charles Perry, warden for twenty years, missed all vestry meetings in 1859 and died in February 1860. It is likely that some of this vestry inertia was due to reluctance to elect new leadership when a revered senior warden was incapacitated or had resigned. When Hackaliah Burt declined to accept reelection as warden at the annual meeting in 1834, the post was left vacant for the following year.

relationship between them but assured him that they understood that he was going to a field of "greater usefulness."

Two months later, after Christmas, the vestry deliberated at great length about the state of the parish and established a committee to find someone to take charge of the parish at a salary of $1200. On this basis they offered the parish to the Rev. Anthony Scuyler, who declined. Approaches to the Rev. Charles H. Platt eventually proved successful and he took office in April of 1860. Once more the rectory underwent repairs. Under Mr. Platt's leadership the painful issue of the pew assessments was confronted and the rate was raised.

As the year 1860 developed it appeared that the depression which had followed the Panic of 1857 was over. In the Midwest the ore furnaces were busy heating the iron for the coming hostilities between the North and the South. St. Peter's vestry experienced a more comfortable level of support for their expenditures. A contract for a new pipe organ was arranged with the Jardine Company of New York at a price of $2000. The vestry found it possible to pay all their bills from the expanding pew rents and subscriptions.

When in 1860 Charles Henry Platt was called to the rectorship of St. Peter's he had already established himself as one of the outstanding clergymen in Western New York. He had been sent to Buffalo by Bishop DeLancey as a new priest in 1845. In Rochester he and the Rev. John Van Ingen had worked together in starting new work. Charles Hayes said of him that he was "one of the most brilliant and capable of our clergy of that day and long after."[7] His wife, Emma Theodosia (Hotchkiss) Platt, came from Lockport, a village with which the Platts

---

[7] Hayes, 177.

had many associations. Their child Clara Hotchkiss Platt was born in St. Peter's rectory on November 20, 1860.

As the Civil War broke out in 1861, Charles Platt made a strong effort to tend to his pastoral duties. He presented 14 for confirmation, and baptized about 20 persons per year. Strangely enough, there were few weddings even as the war began to pull men away for the struggle against secession. He performed 7 marriages in 1860 and 2 in 1861. But his mind was on other matters.

Chaplains were needed for the new regiments forming up throughout New York state. In Rochester Platt's former associate, the Rev. John H. Van Ingen, was mustered in as Chaplain of the 8th (Rochester) Cavalry Regiment on November 23, 1861. At the same time in Auburn, the 75th Infantry Regiment had as its chaplain, the Rev. Thomas B. Hudson, thirty-seven, a Presbyterian minister from nearby Springport.

The thirty-eight year old Platt wasted no time getting into the chaplaincy. The war broke out in April of 1861. With the four companies recruited at Lockport, Mr. Platt was mustered in as Chaplain of the 28th Infantry Regiment New York State Volunteers, the "Niagara Rifles," on May 22, 1861, having volunteered for two years. The vestry accepted his resignation, sadly acknowledging his "brief stay."[8]

The former rector saw duty with his regiment first in the defense of Washington, a position to which many New York units were dispatched for training and in the growing concern that the capitol would be

---

[8] Evidently Platt was not immediately called to full duty. On June 8, 1861, St. Peter's sexton, Truman A. Howden, 24, died of an overdose of laudanum, and his remains, conveyed to Lockport, were interred by Mr. Platt.

FROM TAVERN

overrun by Southern forces. Assigned first to the Army of the Potomac and then to the Army of Virginia, he traveled the Potomac Valley and the Valley of Virginia as far south as Winchester. When his regiment, which fortunately suffered only light losses during the entire war, was once more transferred to the Army of the Potomac in September of 1862 and his period of enlistment was over, he returned home to visit Auburn. There he learned that his services were briefly needed once again.

There had been something tentative in August 1861 about the vestry's decision to engage the Rev. Joseph W. Pierson for only a year at the lower stipend of $1000. However a year later, in April 1862, the vestry formally called him as rector.

The Vestry Minutes reflect very little business in those early war years. In March of 1863 Mr. Pierson's salary was raised to $1200. The vestry purchased four rooms of walnut furniture from him for $300. To meet these expenditures rent was raised on the pews from sixteen percent of their value to twenty percent. William Seward received notice that the rent on his pews numbered 97 and 99 would be increased to forty dollars per annum, each.[9]

Blessed with a raise and paid cash for his own furnishings, the thirty-eight year old clergyman suddenly became tragically ill on Ascension Day, May 14, 1863. Either afflicted by disease brought to Auburn by the gathering recruits, or struck down by a raging sepsis of internal origin, he experienced a violent chill in the morning which led to congestive stupor and death by eleven o'clock the same night. He left

---

[9] Indicating the assessed valuation of his pews at $200 each. Pew rent notice, St. Peter's Church, March 23, 1863. Seward Papers.

behind a widow and three children, one of whom, Ernest DeLancey Pierson, was only six months old.

Mr. Pierson had not had a very active ministry, and unfortunately he was not very punctual in his registry entries. It appears from the parish clerk's later notations that Pierson had about 10 baptisms and 4 weddings per year. Although Bishop DeLancy had visited Auburn in November 1862 to baptize little Ernest DeLancey, there were no confirmations during Joseph Pierson's brief tenure.

Thus, after Charles Platt was mustered out of the army, he was asked to come back to Auburn where he appeared in July and August of 1863 to baptize the grandchildren of General John Chedell and those of the Swains, prominent figures in the parish.[10]

There were another 14 baptisms in two successive weeks in September 1863, administered by a Mr. Rice. One of the young ladies baptized was Miss Frances Seward, aged 19, daughter of William and Frances Miller Seward.[11] These baptisms were later recorded in the strong handwriting of the Rev. John Brainard, whose story with St. Peter's formally began in November, 1863.

---

[10] Charles Platt died in Binghamton, February 25, 1869 at the age of 46. Hayes, 275.

[11] Late baptism seems often the case. Grown and married, Caroline Cornelia Canfield was baptized June 11, 1853. The sponsors were Mrs. Clarence Seward and Mrs. T. G. Howe, Jr. "I was grieved the other day to learn from the neighbors that Caroline had been baptized in our church without saying one word to me on the subject. It is my misfortune to fail to win the confidence of our niece."
FMS to WHS, June 13, 1853.

From Tavern

If we count the list of intentionally resident rectors of Auburn, prior to the coming of John Brainard, there were, starting with John Rudd, nine in all. Of these, four stayed for less than two years, two died in office, one was fired and left angry, and one quite obviously was never serious about the job. Only five could be said to have had a settled ministry, three with six years, one with five and one with four. Three times the parish had been vacant for the period of a year. St. Peter's Church cried out for a faithful pastor who would embrace Auburn and love his work.

A depiction of Secretary William H. Seward, as published in *Harper's Weekly* on April 6, 1861.

Chapter 6

THE SEWARDS AND RELIGION

William Henry Seward was raised in an environment that was religious in a civic sense, but his family seems to have had little specific church orientation. In 1829 his sister Louisa Cornelia joined the Methodist church. When in 1832 his brother George determined to join the Episcopal Church, local Presbyterians in Florida, New York, offered their sympathy to his mother.[12]

When Seward first arrived in Auburn on a Sunday in 1823, he inquired where he might find Judge Elijah Miller who had invited Seward to join him in his law practice. The aspiring lawyer was told to look for the jurist at St. Peter's Episcopal Church on Genesee Street.

On October 20, 1824, William Henry Seward [she always called him Henry] married Frances Adeline Miller in St. Peter's Episcopal Church, Auburn, New York. Miss Miller's family were listed in the church records as belonging to the parish.[13] Her father, Judge Elijah Miller, thought to be of Quaker background, was a vestryman and owned a pew in St. Peter's, as well as one in the Universalist church. Miss

---

[12] "George...is going to unite himself with the Episcopal Church sometime this spring. [He seems] sincere in everything else." His mother was satisfied, but the local Presbyterians consoled her. FMS to WHS, April 19, 1832.

[13] "List of Families belonging to this church," c. 1820, Parish Register No.1.

Miller's mother Hannah Foote passed away when Frances was only seven. After Hannah Foote Miller died of consumption at her mother's home in Williamstown, Massachusetts, in 1809, Judge Miller ceased all relationship with the Footes. Mrs. Miller seems to have played small part in her daughter's life.

Elijah Miller was elected to the vestry of St. Peter's in 1810 and re-elected continually to that responsible body until 1826. In 1811 Judge Miller contributed $200 to the construction of the first church. In 1828 he pledged $50 toward the purchase of the rectory. It is obvious that he was one of the leading supporters of St. Peter's, though it is doubtful that he had ever been baptized and he certainly never became a communicant. His son-in-law Alvah Worden, came from a very devout Episcopalian family, and was elected to the vestry from 1824 until 1826.[14]

Judge Miller's other son-in-law, the rising lawyer William Henry Seward, was elected to the vestry of St. Peter's Church in April of 1827 and took an active part in parish affairs. In 1827 he was chosen as a delegate to the convention of the Diocese of New York. In 1828 he contributed twenty-five dollars toward the purchase of the George Croul house next door to the church for use as a parsonage. That same year when the parish purchased the Brick House and Lot near the corner of James and Genesee he again contributed twenty-five dollars. In 1831 he was active in the move to enlarge the first wooden church. After 1834 he was not present at vestry meetings with any regularity. He declined further election to the vestry in 1836.

---

[14] Alvah Worden, a storekeeper, was the husband of Lizette Maria Miller, and the son of Nathan Worden and Sarah Pulling, the last noted for her strong Episcopalian beliefs. His brother Warren Worden [b.1806] was for a time part of the law practice of Miller and Seward.

In mid October of 1835 the cornerstone was laid for the commencement of the Auburn and Owasco Canal, a $100,000 project designed to raise the level of the lake and to generate water power in the outlet equivalent to seven hundred horsepower. Seward was selected to make the dedicatory address. He chose to mention St. Peter's Church as an example of the truth that the present group endeavor was made easier by the reality that the population of the area had grown to 5,385, and he compared their work with the more difficult labors of the pioneers of the village.

In the beginning, he maintained, the efforts of Colonel Hardenbergh were individual, solitary, and at great cost for those days. But now, he continued:

> Ours is a work of united effort, requiring only surplus capital. I am sure none of my generous fellow citizens will dissent when I add that the venerated William Bostwick and his respected coadjutor Hackaliah Burt evinced a higher sense of the value of religious education by erecting the first Christian Church at Hardenbergh's Corners, than we have done, who of our abundance have since established at Auburn so many costly and splendid houses of worship.[15]

In August of 1838 the distinguished politician was chosen as a member of the committee to decide diocesan boundaries, as the Diocese of Western New York was being divided off from its parent, the Diocese of New York. In October of 1838 Seward was elected as a delegate to the convention of the newly created western diocese in Geneva. In

---

[15] "An Address at the Commencement of the Auburn and Owasco Canal, October 11, 1835." Privately printed, Auburn, 1835.

FROM TAVERN

August of 1845 he was again elected as delegate to convention. After his retirement as Secretary of State he was chosen one final time as delegate to the 1866 diocesan convention.

It is a comment on the practices of the Episcopal Church in Seward's time that he initially exercised such active participation on a parish vestry just by virtue of his prominence and by owning several pews in St. Peter's Church. William Henry Seward was not baptized in the Episcopal Church nor did he become a communicant until May of 1837 when he was 36 years old.

In their family life William Henry and Frances Seward made clear their distaste for any display in religion, and they refused to be intimidated by any 'blue-nosed' tradition in Auburn or elsewhere. Seward was addicted to smoking cigars and he liked playing cards. At their parties they had fiddling and dancing, much to the condemnation of the ardent spirits among the student body of Auburn's Presbyterian Seminary.

In 1831 when a prominent friend called to invite the household to attend the sermons of the revivalist Charles Grandison Finney who was preaching nightly in Auburn, Frances' grandmother Pauline told the surprised visitor that "<u>Seward and his wife</u> did not believe in revivals of this kind."[16]

But later Frances did go to hear Finney out of curiosity, where she developed the opinion that "the man must be crazy." As the evangelist repeated over and over again the phrase 'don't ask God to make you a

---

[16] March 11, 1831, FMS to WHS.

new heart, make yourself a new heart,' she concluded that he was little but a "low comic with a dozen stories."[17]

In late 1834 a crisis developed in the relationship between Henry and Frances Seward. She felt herself neglected by a husband who was so often far from home, and he acknowledged that he had let ambition and worldly activity create a void between them. Writing in the idiom of religion while on a business trip to Albany, he wrote out his desire to be reconciled to her and his penitent adherence to their marriage. "My dearest Frances, I have always loved you, as the best and chiefest of my affections. I have been led afar by ambition which has only this mitigation, that it was neither sordid nor selfish." Choosing religious language to phrase his desire to turn once more to her the remaining energy of his heart he added, "Heaven only knows whether I can become a Christian. That I ought, I know and feel."[18]

Her somewhat stilted, if not catechetical response took note of the requirements of his rational nature but sought to secure him for herself, no matter how far away he might be, by affirming the dual significance of the motions of his heart.

> You say my dear Henry you doubt whether you can become a Christian in such a world as this. We can be Christians anywhere provided God is with us. His grace is sufficient to strengthen us in all seasons of trial, and this is but a world of probation.

---

[17] March 13, and April 13, 1831, FMS to WHS.
[18] Seward Papers, WHS to FMS, December 8, 1834. Quoted in John M. Taylor, *William Henry Seward, Lincoln's Right Hand* (New York: Harper Collins, 1991), 36.

> You say you desire that the change should be wrought in your heart by reason and reflection — reason and reflection <u>alone</u> can produce no such change — does reason and reflection make us love our earthly friends? That would be a cold kind of love which did not permit the heart to have any influence. I too wish your understanding to be convinced but I wish to have your heart converted — this must be done by the influence of God's spirit.

And she assured him that God would answer if he persevered, adding that her own dear Henry should "seek an acquaintance with Him."[19]

It was in this crisis period that the then rector of St. Peter's, the Rev. William Lucas, found opportunity to encourage Frances Seward to become a communicant. Before approaching Frances directly, Lucas had felt obliged to broach this prospect with her husband.

> Mr. Lucas who is a very good man and a good Christian spent an hour with me Tuesday — we had a long and I believe satisfactory conversation on the subject of religion. He is desirous that I should become a communicant in our Church and says that it is not necessary that the rite of confirmation should first be administered. I expressed to him my unbelief in infant baptism — which he said you had mentioned to him — he said he would not attempt to convince me with his own arguments but would send me some books which I promised to read.[20]

---

[19] FMS to WHS, December 14, 1834.
[20] FMS to WHS, January 2, 1835.

After an interval, Frances Seward, as "ready and desirous to be confirmed," was entered on the roll of communicants at St. Peter's on October 18, 1835 and later confirmed by Bishop B. T. Onderdonk. She continued to encourage Henry in believing in his ability to become a Christian. "I think you will and can be a Christian without either the enthusiasm or the remorse which many persons feel and which many consider so essential." And she added, "You have a keen moral sense and an even temper."[21]

Meanwhile their faith and communion was sorely tested. A daughter Cornelia was born to them in the summer of 1836. In September Frances reported to Henry that "our little girl" was taken downstairs for the first time.[22] On December 28, Dr. Erastus Humphreys, their physician and a communicant of St. Peter's, came to pay a Christmas call. The Humphreys and the Sewards were acquaintances and Frances had been confirmed in the same class as two of the doctor's daughters. Naturally the growing infant was examined informally by the doctor, especially as she seemed a bit unwell.

There was "an alarm of smallpox in the village" and on New Year's Day Frances gave thought to sending for Dr. Humphreys to vaccinate the baby, but her Aunt Clary thought it a shame unnecessarily to "make the little creature sick."[23] The child became more obviously ill, vomiting, with eruptions around the throat. The housekeeper pronounced it smallpox. Dr. Humphreys was sent for. He concurred. The infant became covered with eruptions.

---

[21] FMS to WHS, October 16, 1836.
[22] FMS to WHS, September 24, 1836.
[23] FMS to WHS, January 1, 1837.

Frances then recalled that Dr. Humphreys, on his visit after Christmas, had remarked that he had come straight from his old office, where she had strong reason to believe that he had just attended a patient with smallpox. She and her father blamed Humphreys for the child's infection and Judge Miller demanded that she dismiss Humphreys from the case immediately.

The child Cornelia died of the smallpox and was buried in St. Peter's churchyard on January 16, 1837, listed as "Frances, infant of W.H. Seward."[24] The father remained at his workplace in Westfield in Chatauqua County. To him Frances wrote "You spoke…of receiving the sacrament of baptism." He worried that he might be thought affected, and she assured him that he would do the right thing.[25]

The cloud of the baby's death from smallpox hung over the Seward family for months. Taking her son Frederick to visit at a neighbor's home in February, Frances was appalled to overhear the lady say to someone, "That is the little boy who is brother to the child that died with the smallpox." In March Frances reported to Henry that "people still fear contagion by coming to see us."[26]

Hard too was her unavoidable proximity in church to the man who caused her terrible loss. Dr. Humphreys, in his concern at the tragedy, was unable to leave the Sewards alone. When he inquired of Peter, the

---

[24] Thus in the Parish Register, died January 14. Also a death notice, "In this village, on Saturday evening, Frances, daughter of the Hon. Wm. H. Seward, aged about 6 mos." *Cayuga Patriot*, January 18, 1837, p.3, col.1.

[25] FMS to WHS, February 14, 1837.

[26] FMS to WHS, February 24, 1837, March 29, 1837.

Seward's manservant, about news of the family, she termed the doctor's interest "contemptible."[27]

Humphreys persisted. When the unwelcome fellow Episcopalian paid a social call on the new governor's wife a year later on New Year's Day in 1838, Frances complained it gave her a headache. She found him obtruding, unfeeling, unprincipled. "God knows I forgive him the misery and disappointment he caused me, if I did not I could not kneel with him at the same altar, but his presence here distresses me exceedingly."[28]

In early April of 1837 she learned of Henry's baptism on Sunday, March 25, in far away western New York. "I was made very happy yesterday by your letter of last Sunday – the day on which you made an open profession of faith in the religion of our blessed Saviour. May his spirit enlighten your footsteps."[29]

The day that he was baptized Seward wrote a private letter explaining his motives for seeking baptism to his close friend and associate Thurlow Weed. His sense of the appropriateness of the act was so profound that he told the political leader how happy he would be if Weed were to exercise the same "duty."

---

[27] FMS to WHS, August 12, 1838.
[28] FMS to WHS, January 2, 1838.
[29] FMS to WHS, April 2, 1837.

From Tavern

Westfield, Chatauqua Co., Sunday, March 25, 1837.

My dear Weed: I have yours of the 19th. It was written in answer to mine of the date of a fortnight since. Frederick was very ill, and was much reduced, but thanks to the mercy of God, is spared to us. You can have no conception how my heart is bound up in the life of that blessed boy.

I have today, not without fear and trembling, but I trust in sincerity and firmness of purpose, discharged a duty unknown before. For years past I have struggled against prejudices of early education which rendered religion a mystery, and yet carried about me a conviction that it was in reality a simple and beautiful system, the profession and practice of which were obvious duties.

After what, I trust, has been a proper self-examination, I presented myself for baptism, and was received into the visible Church, and for the first time enjoyed the Communion Supper. I mention this fact, which will be inharmonious with your daily thoughts and occupations, because it is an important event in my life, and one which, therefore, you should know directly from me, instead of hearing it by report. If, in one of those seasons (which seldom occur) when you are alone and free from the pressure of immediate care, you remember this circumstance, your intimate knowledge of my recent experience of human events will, I doubt not, enable you to trace the causes and manner of my becoming more serious than heretofore in regard to religion.

If that or other course of thought should lead you to the conviction that what I have done is an obvious and proper duty devolving upon yourself as well as me and all others, it would be a source of great happiness to me. You will not be likely to fall into the error into which others will in respect to myself. But I may as well be explicit with you. I profess not to have experienced any miraculous change of heart, or to have in any way gone through that ordeal of despair so commonly supposed to be the entrance, and the only entrance, upon Christian life. I have always been sensible that I was an offender, and a grievous one, against the duty I owed to God and my fellow men.

I have endeavored now to repent, and resolve, with God's grace, to live more in the fear of and under the influence of love and gratitude to God, and to that end to study His revelation. I do not anticipate that it will make any considerable change in my habits of life, but I humbly trust that it will gradually elevate and refine my motives of action. Commend my love to Mrs. Weed and Harriet.

Ever yours, William H. Seward."[30]

Certainly Seward was moved to baptism by the serious thoughts occasioned by the death of his tiny girl and the illness of his firstborn son. How much he was also inclined to do so by the gathering possibility that he might become Governor, is hard to establish. But the

---

[30] From a newspaper article "Mr. Seward and Mr. Weed" published after Seward's death in October 1872. Pasted in the front of John Brainard's Journal of Official Acts.

statement that he "allowed himself to be baptized in the Episcopal Church" seems not to be merited by the events.[31] Though he enjoyed most of the sins allowed to Episcopalians, as well as some that were not sanctioned, Seward believed that his moral actions and his responses to duty were completed by a convinced and public membership in the Christian church.

He often referred to his milder views as those of one who was "a Whig in politics and an Episcopalian in religion." His political associates made reference to his previous church offices, and Lincoln sometimes poked fun at him. Once, when Lincoln and Seward were riding side by side in a wagon, the mule skinner swore loudly and horribly at the mules. Lincoln, who was sensitive to such things, leaned forward and said to the driver, "Excuse me sir, are you an Episcopalian?" When the astonished driver said no and then asked why the President thought he might be, Lincoln said, "Well, you sound just like Mr. Seward when he is upset."

With Frances fully confirmed in the fall of 1835, Henry was entered in St. Peter's communicant list two years later on September 3, 1837. It was a way that they could be close even with the demands of his career. Both of them could be joined in spirit in the sacrament of the church's altar, though physically far apart.

Frances was often negatively taken with the competitive rigidity of Auburn's Presbyterians, particularly when their blood ran hot at revival time. In March of 1831, at the time of the accusations against Dr. Rudd

---

[31] John M. Taylor, *William Henry Seward, Lincoln's Right Hand* (New York, 1991), 38. In this otherwise excellent study, the author mistakenly refers to "St. Paul's Episcopal Church in Auburn."

made by certain students of the Seminary, when it was demanded of the rector to know whether he had "gone to Mrs. Seward's party where they had fiddling and dancing," she resolved not to attend any more Presbyterian meetings, because of "their insults to the members of our church."[32] In April of that year she remarked on the "numberless emissions" sent out by the Presbyterians to counteract the services in the Episcopal church and said she had been told that Dr. [Joseph T.] Pitney[33] had said no Episcopalians could enter heaven.[34]

Frances' father maintained a pew in Auburn's Universalist church and she grew up in a neighborhood which made it convenient for the Millers to attend services there, at first in a house next door, and then later just across the street. Their early home on South Street had been right between First Universalist Church, on the corner of Grover Street, and the Second Presbyterian. Her sympathetic feelings toward the Universalists, a large congregation in Auburn at that time, found their base in the fact that the Universalist faith in the universal salvation of all mankind was the very antithesis of Presbyterian insistence on the reality of eternal damnation for some. Orestes Brownson, later famed as a Catholic philosopher but then still a Universalist and in his late Brook Farm stage, returned to Auburn to lecture in 1842. Frances and her Aunt Clara went to hear him and determined to take Fred to hear the whole course.[35] On the death of Hosea Ballou in mid 1852, Frances went to hear pastor William L. H. Mellen expound on the passing of the great Universalist divine.[36]

---

[32] FMS to WHS, March 7, 1831.
[33] Deceased 4/20/1853.
[34] FMS to WHS, April 5, 1831.
[35] FMS to WHS, July 29, 1842.
[36] FMS to WHS, June 28, 1852,

FROM TAVERN

A letter and clipping in the Seward papers illuminates the intensity of the feeling of Auburn's orthodox against the tenets of Universalism. In late 1852 Mr. and Mrs. G. F. H. Lawrence, broad minded patrons of charity, proposed to give a musical benefit for the new "Cayuga Asylum for Destitute Children," and to have several ministers, among them Presbyterian, Universalist, and Episcopalian, participate in the religious exercises which were to be a prominent part of the program. In a letter of January 25, 1853 to the Lawrences, the Rev. Mr. Nelson of the First Presbyterian Church declined to "appear before a congregation in any such connection with (Universalist pastor Mellen) as would imply the recognition of him as a Christian minister," stating that "that scheme with which Mr. Mellen is identified," one whose views are "essentially unchristian," "denies what in my view, is *most* essential and fundamental to the system of doctrines taught in the Bible." In Dominie Nelson's view, the Universalists denied the sovereign will of a God who chose to consign to eternal flames those whom he would.

The Rev. Mr. Mellen, learning of the Rev. Mr. Nelson's reply, proceeded on February 13, 1853, to preach a sermon in defense of his position, and to send it to be published in the Auburn newspaper.[37]

Apparently St. Peter's zealous rector of the day, Walter Ayrault, had previously spurned Dr. Mellen's invitation to organize such a union exercise to help the local Orphan's Home. Either the young rector, wary of the Miller/Seward proclivities, in self defense sent Governor William Henry Seward a copy of his letter of rejection or an indignant Dr. Mellen passed it on to the prominent politician. The painfully frank letter, now among the Seward papers, blunt to the point of insult, helps

---

[37] Newspaper clipping "Bigotry or Charity: Which?" found with Ayrault letter of November 10, 1852, in Seward Papers.

us to understand something more about the religious tensions which broad churchwoman Frances and her ambitious husband found unpleasant.

Auburn, Wed., Nov. 10th, 1852.

Mr. Mellen

My dear Sir, I received your note last evening through the post office and would thank you for the <u>courtesy</u> intended by the invitation — but in declining it you will permit me to say that I could never associate myself with you in any enterprise in which you act or appear as a <u>teacher of Christianity</u> in the community, and as such, I gather from the tenor of your note, you wish to be regarded by those whom you expect to meet at your house on Friday — as you sign yourself "<u>Pastor of the Universalist Church</u>."

Regarding as I do the peculiar religious principles and the whole system of Universalism with <u>the utmost abhorrence</u> you will see at once it would be quite wrong and inconsistent to associate myself with you in any way as a clergyman of this city.

But I beg you to understand that while I thus regard your <u>position</u> in the community as just the <u>antagonist</u> and <u>opposite of my own</u> — as teaching for truth what I think to be <u>utterly</u> false — still as a <u>man</u> & a <u>citizen</u> in private life I should always treat you with that courtesy which are [sic] due from a Christian and a gentleman.

> The care & <u>substantial relief</u> of the wants of the poor has always formed one of the principal objects of my calling as Christ's minister and I can assure you it will never be lost sight of.
>
> Declining therefore with the utmost personal kindness all cooperation with you in any such way as you propose, and professing to devote myself to the care of the poor in other ways you will I trust believe me your sincere well wisher.
>
> Walter Ayrault, Rector of St. Peter's Church.

To the mind of the "strong church" young rector, Mellen was denigrating the essentials of the Church by pretending to exercise an office to which he was not apostolically entitled, and for which there was no surety in church order. This was certainly in the line of Hobart "high" churchmanship, though scarcely, one might hope, in terms that the sainted bishop would have chosen.

How or why the letter from Ayrault and the related newspaper clipping found its way into the Seward papers is not clear. Seward was a personal friend of the Rev. John Mather Austin, pastor of the First Universalist Church of Auburn from October of 1844 to June of 1851, and it was to Austin, who had had his own public orthodox opponents, that Seward turned to request a spiritual call on condemned murderer Bill Freeman in his jail cell.[38]

---

[38] "Remarks made to the Universalist-Unitarian Society of Auburn, New York, by Michael J. Cuddy, City Historian, October 20, 1994." In Universalist File, History Room, Seymour Library, Auburn, N.Y.

It was before Ayrault's letter to Mellen, but still within the period in which the subject of Universalist heterodoxy was under local discussion, that Frances Seward learned that there had supposedly been some hesitation on the rector's part to permit her father's funeral from the church. Judge Miller's funeral had taken place in the church on Sunday, November 16, 1851, at two in the afternoon. Rector Ayrault noted in his journal, "First Interment in Fort Hill Cemetery." The following May, on her way back from an extended visit in New York, Frances reported the rumours from home. "As much as I love our church I fear sometimes they will drive me away from it. It seems to have been the town talk this winter that Mr. Ayrault would not venture to have the remains of our honored father taken into the Church until he had consulted the Bishop. (After all he has done for the Church!)"[39]

Was this just a gossipy fabrication, calculated to wound sensitive Frances? Or was there indeed some hesitation on the part of rigid Ayrault to solemnize the rites for one who had probably never been baptized and who showed affection for the Universalist religion and maintained a pew in their edifice? Surely the Judge's fifteen years on the vestry and his many contributions and his ownership of a pew in St. Peter's must have counted for much. But the fact that the rumour circulated at all gives some evidence of the intensity of feeling on the subject.

Later Frances returned to the subject. She went to church with the children on June 6, 1852, and lingered in St. Peter's churchyard to inspect the grave sites. There had been discussion of removing Grandma Pauline Miller's remains to the new Fort Hill Cemetery to be set alongside her son the Judge, and Frances' Aunt Clara was not willing to

---

[39] FMS to WHS, May 22, 1852.

allow it. And Frances added, "There are so many tender recollections associated with our Church that I never enter it after a long absence without a feeling of sadness. There is so much in her liturgy attractive and soothing that I lament more and more the narrow bigotry and intolerant spirit of her clergy, but like all other things of mortal mould she has a mix of good and ill."[40]

Frances and Henry Seward lived in daily connection to Auburn's growing Irish Catholic population. In February of 1837 Seward's relation Jennings[41] came to Auburn to "preach" on a Sunday. He met with other clergymen and asked Frances "would Mr. Lucas join us?" She responded that she presumed Mr. Lucas was a High Churchman (which would interfere with his cooperation), but that he had never discussed the subject with her.[42] Later Peter Miller, the Irish man of all work, maintained that Jennings warred against the Catholic religion, and that that would hurt Mr. Seward in the election.[43]

Peter had served the family from 1826. The maids employed by Frances were frequently Irish, one of whom, "Irish Mary," she let go in 1838 and then took back again, "in hope of improvement." A "Maryann" left with a company of Irish emigrants for Illinois.[44]

When a Roman Catholic bishop came to Auburn in January of 1848, Frances reported to Henry that "my 'maidens in the kitchen' will be absent a lot this week due to the visit of the Bishop." She would go to hear him preach, "but the little church will be overflowing with the sons

---

[40] FMS to WHS, June 6, 1852.
[41] Possibly his brother, Benjamin Jennings Seward, who died in 1844.
[42] FMS to WHS, February 24, 1837.
[43] FMS to WHS, March 4, 1837.
[44] FMS to WHS, April 13, and 20, 1838.

and daughters of the Emerald Isle." It was quite an event for Auburn's Catholics. "The advent of the Bishop has occupied the foreign parts of our family for the last four days. I went to hear him in the town hall." When the prelate paid a call at the Seward home he did not leave his name so she was unaware until later that he had come to see her. "I have not yet been able to hear the name pronounced intelligibly but I think it is Finous (an assistant Bishop of New York.) He spoke amicably on 'other sheep have I...not of this fold.'"[45]

Frances Adeline Miller Seward died in 1865, struck down by the attempt in Washington on her husband's life and the terrible injuries he received. Her funeral in Auburn was attended by a throng of people, many of whom came as a tribute to Secretary Seward. The Rector, Dr. Brainard conducted the service at the church and at the graveside in Fort Hill on June 24, 1865. He recorded as the cause of death, "prostration."

Just a year and a half later on November 3, 1866, it was Dr. Brainard's sad responsibility to conduct the funeral of their daughter Frances Adelaid Seward. The cause of her death was entered as "bilious fever."

From the second occasion this note to Secretary Seward has been preserved:

---

[45] FMS to WHS, January 17, and 24, 1848.

St. Peter's Rectory, Nov. 2, 1866,

My dear Mr. Seward,

I am overwhelmed at the greatness of your loss. In these last years sorrow upon sorrow has come upon you. But He who has afflicted will afford you comfort and bind up your broken heart. I should have been with you last evening to express my sympathy, and learn your plans, but for a troublesome cough which allowed me no rest. I shall call upon you this morning at 10 o'clock, immediately after our morning service. May God bless you, honored sir, with the richest comforts of His grace.

Most truly yours, John Brainard"[46]

Seven years later it again fell to Brainard's lot to officiate at a funeral of greater importance than any before seen in St. Peter's or in Auburn. William Henry Seward died at his South Street home in Auburn, October 10, 1872, and the funeral ceremonies took place in St. Peter's on October 14, 1872.[47]

---

[46] John Brainard to the Hon. William H. Seward, Auburn. November 2, 1866. Seward Papers.

[47] The details about the funeral appeared in the *Auburn Daily Bulletin*, Monday, October 14, 1872, and Tuesday, October 15, 1872. The reporter wrote of St. Peter's that it was the church "of which Mr. Seward was a communicant and for many years a Vestrymen."

The day before the funeral was the Twentieth Sunday after Trinity and Dr. Brainard preached on the death of Governor Seward, taking as his text Matthew 22:32, "God is not the God of the dead but of the living."[48]

The Secretary's remains lay in state in the south drawing room of the Seward home that October Monday morning from nine until one. The line of viewers was received by Mrs. William H. Seward, Jr., assisted, among others, by Mrs. John Bostwick, Mrs. John Chedell, and Warren Worden, Esq.

The formalities began with a service at the home consisting of a prayer by Dr. Brainard. At 2:30 pm the family and the official mourners proceeded from there to the church in a procession of carriages. The short journey occurred in a heavy downpour. Among the many honorary pallbearers were Nelson Beardsley, General John H. Chedell, and Thurlow Weed.

According to the details provided by the *Auburn Daily Bulletin*, St. Peter's was "beautifully draped by a committee" of E. H. Groot, C. A. Smith, and the Misses Kitty Muir, Mary Meachem,[49] Laura Chedell, Janet Pomeroy, Mary Titus, Jessie Knapp, Hattie Knight and Florence Meachem.

> Mr. Seward's pew, the desk, chancel rail, communion table, organ loft and front of the gallery were draped in plain black broadcloth, with intermixed miniature sheaves of

---

[48] Brainard's Journal Entry.
[49] Mr. Groot and Miss Mary Meachem were married the following January 8, 1873.

natural grain. On the communion table stood a beautiful cross of autumn leaves.

The effect of the whole was impressive, and the arrangement in that severe plainness of elegance that only good taste in such matters can dictate.

The flowers which decorated the drawing room at the residence were disposed about the coffin at the church, and were beautifully conspicuous from their white purity in contrast with the drapery of the black.

The church was completely filled to its capacity of over seven hundred people. Serving as ushers were Charles A. Myers, H. D. Titus, Albert Hollister, H.B. Fitch, Henry Ivison and T. W. Meachem. The remains, borne by six family servants, were followed by the clergy, Dr. John Brainard, the Rev. John R. Hale of St. John's Church, Dr. Eliphalet Nott Potter, president of Union College, the Rev. W. D. Doty of Waterloo, and the Rev. Thomas C. Reed of Geneva.[50]

At the opening, the choir, accompanied by the organist, Mr. W. E. Baker, sang the anthem, "Lord let me know mine end." As Dr. Potter read the passage from First Corinthians , chapter fifteen, verses 20 and following, at the words "it is raised in glory," the sun broke forth through the rain and streamed through the west transept window directly upon the coffin.

---

[50] "Oct. 14, 1872. The funeral of W.H. Seward was attended this day from St. Peter's Church. An immense throng of people in Church and through the city. Day rainy; present of the clergy, with me Drs. Reed and Potter, Hale and Doty." Brainard Journal Entry.

Dr. Brainard announced a departure from the printed program, substituting Hymn 187 "I would not live always," for the previously designated Hymn 183 set to the tune of "Home Sweet Home." In his sermon the rector spoke of William Henry Seward as one who had often at communion "knelt at this altar, until infirmity rendered it impossible to commemorate the passion of his Redeemer."

For those who had not had a previous opportunity to make their farewell, at the close of the service in the church there was a last viewing of the body by "a tremendous multitude." The large crowd who had stood outside in the rain were allowed to come in by the main front entrance and leave by way of the west side door. Shortly after 4:30 the remains were taken from the church to Fort Hill cemetery, where Dr. Brainard conducted the remainder of the burial office. Seward's son Frederick cast the first handful of earth upon the coffin.

The vestry of St. Peter's Church, meeting later that same day to consider a number of important matters relating to the completion of the new church building and the extinction of the debt incurred for it,[51] took sorrowful note of the fact that in the "death of our late distinguished neighbor and friend whose funeral we had this day attended, we had been called upon to part with one of our oldest parishioners as well as one who had served faithfully on our Vestry, and that some action of the Board would be eminently proper." At a meeting on the following evening a committee composed of the rector, William Allen and John Knapp presented this resolution.

---

[51] This was the very moment when General Chedell offered to pay for the completion of the tower and spire and to contribute an additional ten thousand dollars toward extinguishing the debts, provided the vestry would raise another six thousand dollars from the parishioners.

From Tavern

> Whereas it hath pleased Almighty God to remove from this Church one of its oldest and the most distinguished of its members, William H. Seward, who for many years was a communicant and one of the officers thereof,
>
> And whereas the Rector, Wardens and Vestry desire to place on the records of the Church the testimonial of their appreciation of the value, of the great example of his life, and the distinguishing honor such a life has conferred upon it,
>
> Therefore Resolved that we recognize in the faithful and unswerving fidelity to conviction of duty, exhibited on all occasions of his eventful and remarkable career the highest qualities of Christian heroism — having all the elements of character, depth of conviction and an unswerving and heroic adherence thereto which characterized and immortalized the old martyrs, [sic]
>
> Resolved that these proceedings be entered upon the records of this parish and a copy of them signed by the officers of the Church, be sent to the family of the deceased.

Bishop Huntington had been invited to participate in the obsequies, but was prevented by his obligations. His letter to Dr. Brainard was passed on to the Seward family.

Syracuse, Oct. 26, 1872

My dear Brother,

Having just returned from a pressing and absorbing series of visitation journeys — ending with the dedication of St. John's School Building yesterday — I take this opportunity to acknowledge your kind courtesy, and that of the family of the lamented statesman, Mr. Seward, in inviting me to be present at the funeral ceremonies. A reply at the time was rendered impracticable, as you are aware, by my absence in Jefferson Co. The trains on the Monday after the funeral did not enable me to reach Auburn in season for the mournful services. I have read every thing relating to them with the greatest interest, and especially a report of your own feeling and tender discourse in the Church on Sunday.

One of the leading figures of our American history has vanished. His last work remains. Let us be devoutly thankful that he bore his testimony to the Christian Faith which is the only Hope of Nations or of his individual love, and to the Church of Christ which we love.

I beg you to offer to the members of his extended household my most cordial sympathies in their sorrow, and my highest esteem. How changed their home must be!

Faithfully, F. D. Huntington"[52]

---

[52] F.D. Huntington to John Brainard, October 26, 1872. Seward Papers.

From Tavern

Seward's contemporaries, his church associates, found no difficulty in assessing his sense and performance of obligations as deriving from his conviction that it was his duty to profess the Christian religion, and to practice it in the Episcopalian manner.

On the Sunday in 1901 nearest the centennial of Seward's birth Dr. Brainard's sermon was devoted to the Governor's relationship to St. Peter's. He rehearsed how the young lawyer came first to the church and saw the Millers "over the box stove" on Christmas Day in 1822 and how Seward had formally united with the Episcopal Church in March of 1837. From his own experience he spoke of Seward's "regular and devout attendance" and how at church he "seemed to enjoy the salutations of his friends and neighbors, particularly when his absence from home had for some time deprived him of the privilege of occupying the family pew." And, he testified, "It was stimulating and helpful to a preacher and especially to a youthful one to receive the attention which he always gave to the Gospel Message. It would make a small man feel enlarged to have those wonderful eyes fixed upon him from the text to the ascription in constant searching gaze."

John H. Chedell

Chapter 7

THE GREAT PATRON, JOHN H. CHEDELL

The most important lay person to take an active part in the life of St. Peter's in the third quarter of the nineteenth century was General John Hatch Chedell. He was born in the Tolland County area of the state of Connecticut on April 26, 1806. His father Rufus Chedell [originally Cheadle] (1769-1816), and his mother Mary Hatch were married in 1790. John had two older sisters, Laura (1790-1869) and Asenath (1794-1885).[1] When he was ten their father Rufus died and John and his mother and sisters moved to Otsego County, New York, in the bleak winter of 1817-1818. For a year and a half John attended a local academy at Hartwick. At the age of twelve he went to work in a country store as a clerk and at fourteen he apprenticed himself to William Nichols of Cooperstown to learn the watch and silversmith trade. In 1827 at the age of twenty-one he came to Auburn, and set up in the business of watchmaker, silversmith and jeweler, an enterprise which he conducted himself until 1851.

In January 1828 John Chedell married Melita Cook, the middle sister of the five daughters of Philip Cook, at that time a resident of Bath in Steuben County, New York. This union with the Cook family played a significant part in Chedell's life as well as in the life of St. Peter's Church.

---

[1] Asenath married Charles Eldridge Avery in 1829.

FROM TAVERN

John H. Chedell was a natural and practical businessman possessed of great energy, and he actively pursued any matter that he began. His greatest personal asset was his integrity, an integrity that quickly inspired trust. His increasing prosperity was obvious and in a few years he was selected to contract for railroad development on sections of the New York and Erie Railway. In 1829 he was designated Quartermaster for the Thirty-third Artillery, Auburn's local militia. In 1852 he was made a trustee of the new Fort Hill Cemetery and was that same year designated as the first trustee for the Cayuga Asylum for Destitute Children. In 1857 he was commissioned brigadier general in the New York State militia. At the outbreak of the Civil War in 1861 he was again made Quartermaster, this time of the Nineteenth Regiment of volunteers. At the same moment he was appointed the trustee for the $4000 fund raised for the families of the volunteer soldiers. In 1861 he served as Sheriff of Cayuga County.

His acumen showed itself early in the development of the Auburn and Syracuse Railroad which had been chartered in 1834. Capitalized at $400,000 and with Judge Elijah Miller as its president, the venture was completed in 1838 as a wood-railed horse-drawn railway and was converted to steam the following year. During his entire career he was a significant investor in railroads,[2] especially the New York Central and Hudson River Railroad, but also in lines like the Lake Shore and Michigan Southern. Sometime during Erastus Corning's tenure as President of the New York Central Railroad (1853-1864), John Chedell was made a director of the railroad in keeping with Corning's policy of

---

[2] A modern writer estimates that Chedell invested in eleven different railroads. Scott Anderson, "Entrepreneurs and Place in Early America; Auburn, New York 1783-1880," unpublished doctoral dissertation, Syracuse University, 1997, 250.

having experienced 'local' directors from the several regions of the line.[3] At his death he was a prime shareholder of the Oswego Starch Company, a burgeoning enterprise which brought substantial wealth to a group of Auburn investors.[4] He invested in store property in Auburn.[5] His will mentions several stores which he left to his grandchildren. He purchased wax figures from a traveling show which ran out of money in Auburn and with them initiated his museum at 73 Genesee Street.

His sound business judgment was recognized by many banks which chose him as a director. Though he lived in Auburn, in 1866 he was elected President of the Syracuse National Bank.

John Chedell's association with St. Peter's was made firm by his connection in marriage with the staunchly Episcopalian Cook sisters, the children of Philip Cook of Bath. Clarissa (b.1796), Rosamond (b.1806), Melita (b. 1808) and Celuta (b.1809), were the progeny of Philip Cook's first marriage, and a baby sister, Asenath (b. 1829), was the child of Philip Cook's second marriage to wife Rebecca.

Clarissa Cook Hiser bore a daughter Maria Clarissa Hiser in 1818. Rosamond Cook married Gerrit V. Orton. Sister Celuta never married, and the youngest sister Asenath married Edwin P. Hiser about 1850.

John Chedell and Melita Cook were married in 1828. After their second child was born in 1831, Melita Cook Chedell was presented for

---

[3] Auburn *Daily Bulletin*, June 24, 1875. The practice was abolished by Cornelius Vanderbilt.
[4] Among them the Willard family, and the Alonzo G. Beardsley family.
[5] Anderson, *op.cit.*, states that Chedell owned $ 43,000 in store property alone in 1875, 329.

confirmation by the Rev. John Rudd.[6] In 1833 her sister Celuta Cook was also confirmed.

The vestry records show that J. H. Cheadell [sic] was the holder of Pew No. 52 in April of 1838. The pew's fairly high number shows that it had been rather recently purchased. It was valued at $160, a little more than the average seating.

John H. Chedell was elected to the vestry of St. Peter's for the first time on April 12, 1841. His brother-in-law, Gerrit V. Orton, husband of his wife's sister Rosamond, was elected at the same time. Chedell was immediately put to work on the ever vexing problem of the nature of the pew 'ownership.' Later that year he was named to the committee to raise a subscription for the rector's salary.

In 1841 the enterprising hardware merchant offered to install a Nott Stove in the church vestibule, and initially obtained the vestry's approval of the necessary hole in the church wall to complete the installation. The Nott Stove was the invention of the versatile Eliphalet Nott (1773-1866), longtime president of Union College and self-styled 'caloric philosopher.' A tall mass of mounting cast iron boxes, the stoves burned anthracite coal, which must have been attractive to Chedell, a pioneer of the Erie Lackawanna Railroad. The innovation was too much for the vestry, either out of consideration for the wall, or perhaps because wood was cheaper. In any event Chedell was told to desist, and the newfangled contraption was set aside.

---

[6] When the child Jane Elizabeth died at the age of 14 months in 1832, the burial was in the North Street burial ground.

He was not re-elected to the vestry in 1842, nor was his brother-in-law Orton who waited until 1843 to get back on the board. But thereafter either Chedell or Orton were members of the governing body as the vestry struggled with the tenure of the Rev. Samuel Hanson Coxe. Reporting at the annual meeting in March of 1845 for the committee to find ways to pay off the obligation of the rectory mortgage, Chedell proposed a simple subscription, a direct canvass of the pewholders which invited them to pledge amounts without relation to the value of their pews. After a very protracted discussion, the peril of bringing complicated issues to an annual meeting at which any pewholder and contributor could speak, Chedell's plan was accepted, with the proviso that a list of pewholders with a 'theoretical' pro-rated assessment of each would be circulated. Whether this latter provision was intended to hold the feet to the fire of the owners of the high priced pews, or what else, is not clear. That the discussion was allowed to wander that far from the immediate issue may have been one of the smaller complaints against Mr. Coxe.

Chedell served with William Seward in 1845 as a delegate to the diocesan convention in Rochester. Chedell and Orton both continued to deal with the dispatch of Coxe. In apparent good health, Orton was faithful in vestry attendance all through the fall of 1846, attending the session on November 12th. But on November 18th, Gerrit V. Orton, Esq., unexpectedly died.[7]

General Chedell was again elected to the vestry at the annual meeting in April 1847, as was Samuel Blatchford,[8] another lawyer in place of

---

[7] He is buried in the rear of St. Peter's churchyard, where the family plot is marked by an obelisk.

[8] Later a Justice of the Supreme Court of the United States.

Orton, and William C. Beardsley, a banker.[9] John Chedell played an active part in the work of enlarging the church during Walter Ayrault's ministry. In 1854 he was elected as warden for the first time. For several years thereafter he alternated between the post of warden and vestryman.

In connection with that first election as warden he was also confirmed and became a communicant in 1854, a rare event in those times for a man of his public and business stature. But he had been elected to the vestry steadily since 1841 and for a man of John Chedell's known habit of pursuing things with energy, the move was characteristic. Certainly by the date of John Brainard's election as rector and the subsequent warm welcome for him in November 1863, General John Chedell was the most prominent active lay figure at St. Peter's.[10]

His predominantly female family made him a natural spokesman on the vestry for the interests of the "ladies of the parish." In March of 1863 he carried word to the vestry that the "ladies of the parish," i.e., the Cook sisters and nieces, wished to have the kneeling cushion at the chancel rail widened by four to five inches, and that they would pay for the alterations of the step and the cushion. The vestry solemnly agreed to this enlargement, without any mention of the delicate problem that it reflected. In 1863 the fashion of the hoop skirt had conquered Auburn and it was difficult for a wearer to kneel for communion if there was not space enough in front into which to rest the hoops and thus to prevent a revelation of limbs and laces.

---

[9] The 1857 Auburn Directory lists William C. Beardsley as "Cashier, Auburn Exchange Bank, residence 84 South St."

[10] W.H. Seward was occupied with politics, Governor Throop was retired from active life, and Samuel Blatchford, later a Justice of the Supreme Court, was busy with a prominent practice.

At the time of the calling of John Brainard as rector, Chedell served on the committee to make arrangements to house the new couple and to repair the rectory for their use. From that moment on the "General" never faltered in his support for the young rector from Connecticut. Within five years the project of building a new church was underway, encouraged by the liberal gifts[11] of the railroad director/ starch investor/ bank director/ businessman in hardware, silverware, and jewelry, and landholder *in extenso*. After the church proper was completed in 1870, Chedell paid for the construction of the imposing tower attached to the southeast corner. At the end of his life in 1875 he left ten thousand dollars to St. Peter's to clear off the mortgage which had been placed on the rectory to finance the last stage of church construction. Having contributed a corner lot on East Genesee Street for a future St. John's Church, he entrusted a further ten thousand dollars to St. Peter's vestry to see that St. John's would be built. Paragraph 17 of his will[12] states that it was the "warmest wish of my beloved deceased wife" to establish a home for the worthy poor and friendless members of St. Peter's Church Parish, and for which he left an unspecified amount to be administered by Dr. Brainard and others.[13]

His affection for John Brainard is spelled out in his will. Paragraph 13 reads: "To Rev. John Brainard a token of esteem and respect for him as a minister of the gospel and a Christian gentleman, $200 per annum as long as he is rector," one-half for charities and one-half for his personal use.

---

[11] In some remarks made in 1899 Dr. Brainard estimated that General Chedell gave in excess of forty thousand dollars toward the total costs of church and tower.

[12] Liber "Y" (1875-1877), Cayuga County Records Retention Office.

[13] Apparently nothing came of this idea. The specific amount was left blank in the will.

Over the years it was Chedell who proposed the periodic increases in the rector's stipend. In early April of 1869 in the midst of the major church construction, the Rev. John Brainard received a tempting call from St. Paul's Church of New Haven, Connecticut. To avert the loss of their promising pastor, Chedell composed an encomium and plea to the rector to remain, in which the vestry vowed undying support and offered a raise. (And six weeks vacation!) The memorial set the tone for forty more years of Brainard's ministry in Auburn.

> Whereas, we are advised that effort is being made to induce the Rector of this Parish to remove to a church in New Haven, Conn.,
>
> Resolved: that our Rector, the Rev. John Brainard, has the united respect and confidence of this Vestry, and we are assured has in an eminent degree, the respect, confidence and love of all the members of the Church and Parish; that no minister could be more acceptable to his people, and that the interests of the Parish would greatly suffer by his withdrawal; and we hope and trust that he will continue our Rector, and that nothing may occur so long as his life shall be spared, to induce him to resign the position he now holds and so ably fills.
>
> Resolved: That with the completion of our new Church (which we trust will be during the current year) and the additional accommodations and attractions it will afford together with the rapid growth of Auburn and increase of its population, a field for usefulness will be opened to Mr.

Brainard for the exercise of all his zeal and powers which we think will equal all his reasonable aspirations."[14]

When construction of the new church slowed in July of 1869 General Chedell was given power by the vestry to hire as many men as necessary to speed up the completion. From that time until his death the General was concerned to finish the church projects he had furthered in Auburn. At the beginning of August of 1870 he commissioned the purchase of a large stone baptismal font to be decorated with the name of his son William Edward. When the young man died shortly thereafter the vestry gratefully dedicated the wheel window in the rear of the new church to William Edward Chedell.

John Chedell and John Brainard had much in common. Not only did both start out in Connecticut, "that hive of population." Not only did they embody the spirit of growth and progress of the era. For in spite of the success which came to them, both lost wife and child to the great scourge of the time, consumption, tuberculosis, the "White Death."

While the new church was being constructed in that spring and summer of 1869 John Brainard's wife Marie Antoinette was in the last stage of consumption. When her second son Edward Shelton Brainard entered this world on June 6, 1869, the relief-giving upward pressure of the child in her womb on her tubercular lungs, the 'natural pneumothorax' of a later understanding, was taken away by his birth and her condition rapidly worsened. Unable to produce from her wasted body enough natural sustenance for the child, she and her mother attempted to feed the infant by hand. In the midst of summer's heat the baby developed the "cholera infantum" of the time, a bacterial infection which

---

[14] Vestry Minutes, April 13, 1869.

produced cholera-like symptoms and was uniformly fatal.[15] Young Edward Brainard died on August 27, 1869, and his weakened mother gave up the struggle with consumption a month later on October 1.

John Chedell understood very well the particular grief of his younger friend. For he too had lost children in infancy, and consumption was the prevailing cause of death in the Chedell household.

Mary Clarissa Chedell, the first child of Melita and John, was born in 1830. She lived to the age of twenty. In 1850 she married Delon Hinman on June 13, and died of consumption six months later on December 5.[16]

The second child, Jane Elizabeth Chedell, was born in 1831, and died at the age of fourteen months.

The third child, Jane Hobart Chedell, was born in 1833, married in 1856 and bore four children. She died of consumption at 39 in 1872.

The fourth child, John Chedell, was born in 1834, served two years in the Union army and, married in 1863, became the father of two children. He died of consumption at 38 in 1872.

---

[15] A major cause of infant death in the late 1800s, it was also known as "weaning brash," and was associated with hot weather and hand feeding, i.e., not with breast milk. "Pepto-Bismol" was invented to alleviate its symptoms.

[16] Delon Marcus Hinman, having previously moved to New York, died in New Orleans in 1857, aged 32. The place of death and his age suggest that he was on a search for a cure for consumption. It took a month for his remains to reach Auburn. (Auburn *Daily Advertiser*, April 22, 1857.)

The fifth child, Charles Cook Chedell, was born in 1837. He died at age three in January 1840.

The sixth child, Laura Chedell, born in 1840, married William M. Williams on December 4, 1873, at the age of 33 and bore two daughters, Laura Melita and Laura Chedell, the first in 1878 and the second in 1879. One year later Mrs. Laura (Chedell) Williams died at age 40 in 1880, cause of death unstated.[17]

The seventh child, William Edward Chedell, born in January of 1847, died of consumption at age 23 in 1870. He did not marry.

The mother of these seven children, Melita Cook Chedell, died on March 11, 1874, aged 66. Her death was from consumption.

The general passed from this life on June 19, 1875, aged 69. His health had been feeble ever since the death of his wife.[18] He was survived only by his daughter, Mrs. Laura Chedell Williams; a daughter-in-law, Mrs. Charles A. Smith (John Chedell's remarried widow); and six grandchildren. His sister-in-law, Celuta Cook, who lived in the general's home for years, remained free from consumption and continued on to the ripe old age of 80.

In the few years between the completion of the new church and the end of his life in 1875, General Chedell continued to urge the completion of unfinished business. In 1872 he challenged the vestry to pay off the remaining debt by offering to build the bell tower at his own expense

---

[17] But within the likely parameters of consumption. Half of its victims died between 20 and 40.
[18] Auburn *Daily Bulletin*, June 21, 1875.

if the vestry would satisfy the mortgage placed on the rectory. At the same time he gave the corner lot on the East Hill for a church for the new St. John's congregation and placed ten thousand dollars for that construction in the hands of St. Peter's vestry, until the new congregation should actually build.

Excursus V:
The Oswego Starch Company

In 1842, Thomas Kingsford, an Englishman then living in New Jersey, invented a process of making starch, previously made from wheat, out of the copiously available American foodstuff, corn. In 1848 a group of venture capitalists from Auburn persuaded him to develop a factory upstate and the Oswego Starch Company was incorporated. "Kingsford's Silver Gloss" starch began to be manufactured in Oswego, New York, a port village on Lake Ontario.

By the year 1850, corn starch, developed primarily for laundry purposes, was also being packaged for food use. The demand for starch for cooking and for industry rapidly increased. From stiffening the collars and shirts and sheets of prosperous nations to thickening the blanc mange and desserts of the better fed, the need for starch marched on. Textile manufacturing and paper treatments demanded increasing amounts of starch.

The plant at Oswego was enlarged seven times. It began in 1848 with an investment of $50,000 in capital and seventy employees. In 1870 it was said to be the most extensive starch factory in the world, producing twenty-one tons a day and employing five hundred men. By 1880 it was the largest factory of its kind in the world. "Silver Gloss" Starch sold all over the United States and in Great Britain. At the height of production it is estimated that it employed 1,000 to 1,100 workers in over twenty acres of interior floor space. Production peaked at thirty-six tons of starch each day. It took five million board feet of lumber annually to make the shipping boxes. And though Thomas Kingsford was billed in the company advertising as the "sole inventor of a process to make starch from Indian corn," plenty of competition developed for the Oswego firm. One hundred and forty other starch factories competed with it by 1879, as American starch output doubled between 1869 and 1904.

The location at Oswego was ideal for the manufacture of starch, an industry which required lots of coal, water and corn. The factory used water from the lake and had a port to which could be delivered the enormous quantity of coal needed to generate the steam required for the wet-milling process. The wooded hills of upstate New York supplied the lumber for the boxes. But most importantly, the great fertile plain south of Lake Ontario produced the huge supply of maize, corn, which was the principal ingredient.

The company was a remarkable example of the ability of American firms after the Civil War to "exploit the continuous improvements in transportation and communication, achieving important economies in large-scale production and distribution" and to ship product into a growing national and international market.[1] It was the first of its kind to achieve mass production, to gain market power through mass advertising, to develop a large export trade, and to employ automatic machinery.[2]

Thomas Kingsford died in 1869 and the company passed into the direction of Thomson Kingsford, his son, who lived until 1900. From its inception until its transfer of ownership in 1902 to the National Starch combine, a group of Auburn citizens were heavily rewarded by

---

[1] Corn Annual 2000, www.Corn.org [7/27/02], Brian W. Peckham.
[2] *Ibid.*

their practically exclusive participation in the new industry. Sylvester Willard and Erastus Case had made contact with Kingsford in New York City and persuaded him that Auburn could provide the venture capital necessary to finance a large establishment in Oswego. Willard and Case backed the operation primarily, and Alonzo G. and Nelson Beardsley became the watchdogs of the investment. General Chedell was also a significant investor. Together the investors supplied the original $50,000 for the start up in Oswego, with Case the largest stockholder.[3]

The money to and from the operation of the Oswego Starch factory flowed through Auburn. In the Rare Book, Manuscript and Special Collections Library of Duke University there is a large collection titled the "Alonzo G. Beardsley Papers." These documents consist mainly of fragments from the correspondence of a law firm whose partners were Theodore M. Pomeroy, William Allen, and Alonzo G. Beardsley.

Included in the collection are a number of items which relate to Beardsley's role as treasurer of the starch enterprise. A memo dated February 1, 1858, from some previous treasurer, instructs the lawyer Beardsley in the duties of his office. "Send Tho. Kingsford every Monday for current expenses $1,000, and as this don't quite pay…send more occasionally." Beardsley was instructed to be lenient in collecting from the laundresses in Troy and out of state. At this rate the expenses of the firm seem to have been $55,000 to $60,000 per year.

---

[3] The most complete account of the rise of the Oswego Starch Company is to be found in Scott Anderson's, "Entrepreneur and Place in Early America; Auburn, New York 1783 – 1880," unpublished doctoral dissertation, Syracuse University, 1997.

From Tavern

The arrangement appears to have been that Kingsford ran the operations of the actual plant in Oswego and looked after sales and advertising. Customer relations and shipping, the financial and stockholder relations offices, especially that of Secretary and Treasurer, were in Auburn, where the cash flow was controlled by the Beardsleys on behalf of the board of directors.

In February, 1859, James W. Simonton of Washington, DC, was having trouble selling his five shares of starch stock. Simonton wrote that he had no idea of parties who held or dealt in it, "beyond my own little circle of Auburn friends." In April of the same year George Underwood of New York, inquiring about the starch dividend, was uncertain how many shares he owned, perhaps as many as sixty. By September of 1859 James Simonton, needing money, had pledged his five shares of stock, for which he claimed to have paid a thousand dollars, for four hundred dollars to William Burr. Burr wrote to William Allen in Auburn, saying he did not want to own the stock as he did not live in Auburn or know anything about the affairs of the company. The shares were eventually sold by Simonton for $497.00.

From these careful beginnings the company made steady progress. In February 1863 Alonzo Beardsley wrote to Congressman Theodore M. Pomeroy, "We should show a very satisfactory result of the year's business at Oswego. I passed all of the last winter at that place."

In March 1863, E. N. Kellogg ("Agent in New York for Oswego Starch") wired Beardsley "Send fourteen hundred (1400) each size handbills to Howe Utica by express tonight." One hundred ninety-six Fulton Street in New York was listed as the "Central Agency of the Oswego Starch Factory," from which E. N. Kellogg remitted payments to Beardsley in Auburn.

In February 1864 Treasurer Beardsley was rewarded with a ruling from the U.S. Treasury Department that "the government makes no direct claim on the company" of any revenue tax upon a dividend declared by the managers of the Oswego Starch Company. Individual recipients of the dividends were responsible for any income taxes. Thus the profits of the company could be passed on to the stockholders without diminution.

These profits can be estimated from a statement, if typical, of income and expenditures for the month of September 1869. The Oswego Starch Company had expenses that month of $106,872.14 against receipts of $134, 398.64.

A burgeoning Oswego Starch Company was represented with a display at the Philadelphia Centennial Exhibition in 1876. A newspaper of the time carried their lengthy publicity statement showing that the officers in Auburn, were Dr. S. Willard, President; Nelson Beardsley, Vice-President; Alonzo G. Beardsley, Secretary and Treasurer; and listed "T. Kingsford and Son, Manufacturers." The full Board of Directors included the officers and Thomas Kingsford, as well as E. B. Morgan, T. M. Pomeroy, William Allen, William H. Seward, Jr., and C. H. Merriman. Most of these were Auburnians, and at least two were members of St. Peter's, Seward Jr. and William Allen. The three sons of Alonzo Grover Beardsley, William Porter, Alonzo Grover II, and Douglas, were baptized in St. Peter's.

William Allen (born 1817), Alonzo G. Beardsley's law partner, was a very active vestryman and significant supporter of St. Peter's Church. Elected to the vestry in 1862, he was re-elected nineteen times and remained a member until his death in January 1881. His memorial in the vestry minutes, composed by David M. Osborne, says of Allen that "his [law] practice ... was large, lucrative, and eminently successful." Described as a "man of affairs," Allen was instrumental in the erection of the new St. Peter's in 1868-1870, having proposed that the firm of Dudley and Dudley be engaged to design the work.

Though not still enlarged to its final condition, the Oswego plant was described in 1876 as "seven stories high, ...with 689 cisterns or vats with a capacity of 3, 150,000 gallons of water, 48 pumps, ... five miles of shafting, ...and ten steam engines of 845 horsepower." It burned 6,000 tons of coal and used 701,000 pounds of paper and five million board feet of lumber each year.

By 1882 the company letterhead still listed "S. Willard (Auburn)," as President and Alonzo G. Beardsley as Treasurer, but added Alonzo's son, William P. Beardsley, as "Assistant Treasurer."

In 1893 a bejeweled "Indian Queen" and her accompanying eagles adorned a twelve-page souvenir starch booklet for the Columbian Exposition in Chicago, provided by Kingsford and Son, Oswego, New York.

For the directors and investors the starch business was a happy combination with their investments in banks, railroads, and other industries. Alonzo Beardsley's records show that he also controlled a business which supplied elm lumber to Oswego Starch, to a wagon factory, and to a wheelbarrow factory. In addition he sold cordwood to the Rome, Watertown and Ogdensburg Railroad.

Scott Anderson states that by 1875 an original investment in Oswego Starch had substantially multiplied.[4] General Chedell's 1875 will conveyed multiple shares of Oswego Starch to each legatee, and consigned other blocks to his executors to be held in trust. Anderson found that each share was paying a generous twenty per cent dividend.

Auburn's interrelated capital is underlined in the marriage in 1885 of the nineteen year old Mary Augusta Chedell, the daughter of the late John Chedell, and granddaughter of the late General, to Douglas Beardsley, son of Alonzo Glover Beardsley, the Treasurer of the Oswego Starch Company. When Alonzo G. Beardsley retired, another of his sons, William Porter Beardsley, became Treasurer and remained in that position until the sale of the company after the turn of the century.

The buildings of the original starch factory burned in February of 1904.[5] The next October A.P. Murdoch and Karl Kellogg of Oswego, and William Porter Beardsley of Auburn, formed the Oswego Maize Product Company, capitalized at $200,000, to resume the manufacture of starch, using certain patents developed by Mr. Murdoch during his previous association with the Oswego Starch Company. The Auburn *Daily Advertiser*, in an article headed "To Buck The Trust," commented on the fact that William P. Beardsley had succeeded his father as treasurer of the old company and asserted, not totally correctly, that either he or his father had been treasurer since Oswego Starch incorporated in 1848.[24]

---

[4] Anderson, *op. cit.*
[5] Auburn *Daily Advertiser*, Feb. 22, 1904.
[24] *Ibid.*

St. Peter's Church, Auburn, New York
Consecrated, October 18, 1870

Chapter 8

WOMEN AND ST. PETER'S

An examination of St. Peter's Church, today still much as it was rebuilt and enlarged in 1870, shows unmistakably that the decoration of the interior is influenced by gender. There is a "distaff side" and a "spear side."[1] The stained glass windows on the right (the east side), said to be "after Overbeck," are all of men, some of whom are carrying spears or staves.[2] The windows on the left side of the church, begin with androgynous angels in the transept and thereafter represent women and women's subjects.[3] Not only the figural windows, but the theme windows have to do with the concerns of women. Moving left from the angelic musicians over the side door, we come to a scene showing our Lord comforting three female mourners. The 1955 Anonymous[4] chose to see three Marys here, the Virgin standing, Mary of Bethany kneeling, and identified the third figure, with the unbound hair of grief, as Mary Magdalene. But the inscription below from the Beatitudes makes it clear that the scene depicts mourners in general. The second half of the window depicts the institution of the Lord's

---

[1] "Spear side" seems to be the accepted opposite of "distaff side."
[2] Friedrich Overbeck, the early 19th Century founder of the "Nazarene" school, made notable use of spears and staves in his larger works as lines of force and containment.
[3] Of course they are archangels, after Fra Angelico, but the fluted robes, conventional in art to indicate heavenly creatures, make them appear feminine.
[4] The sesquicentennial booklet, with its extensive section on the windows, has no identified author.

From Tavern

Supper, in the nineteenth century frequently described as the "nutritive" sacrament.

Again moving to the left we observe two female figures, described in the accounts of 1870 as Resignation (with uplifted eyes), and Temperance.[5] Later analysts have wanted Resignation to be the Virgin Mary, based largely on the lilies below. But lilies, flowers of purity, were used in many of these windows. The Temperance figure to the left has also been called St. Margaret of Scotland, based on the thistles below, but they surely are a reference to the Scottish origin of the Muirs, the donors of the window.

The next pair of figures shows Faith, with a wooden cross, and Hope, touching the traditional anchor. The inscription, "Her children rise up and call her blessed," emphasizes the female aspect of these theological virtues.

The next window shows gleaning Ruth, a good and faithful woman of the Hebrew scriptures, who finds at last in Boaz a faithful husband. It is joined by the New Testament scene in which Jesus speaks prophetically at the well to the Samaritan woman, who had five or six unfaithful husbands.

Finally, at the end of the western wall, there is another group of mourners, representing the Patience and Devotion of the aged and the widows and the orphans of the 1860's, in post-war Auburn, a community which lost so many of its sons and fathers to the War Between the States.

---

[5] Description in a lengthy newspaper article published the day of the consecration, Oct.18, 1870. Brainard scrapbook.

An understanding of the broader meaning of these portrayals of mourning, sorrow, and resignation, is informed by recalling some themes of mind and spirit of the period in which they were erected. The virtue of Resignation, for example, was one of the fixations of nineteenth century literature, which saw an edifying significance in the slow death of so many youths of the time from deadly "consumption," tuberculosis. In 1829 the Editor of the *Gospel Messenger,* John Rudd, remarked upon the spiritual "beauty" of the consumptive female which shone forth as the progression of the disease brought out devotion and tenderness, a piety, a growing <u>resignation</u> on the part of the dying invalid.[6]

Young Arthur Cleveland Coxe, on a fine June Sunday in 1835, taking advantage of his Presbyterian father's absence from Auburn, attended St. Peter's services. Overcome with the emotion of a country Sabbath, he observed the persons pouring into the church.

> Here a venerable couple with their gay young daughters, each carrying her prayer-book neatly folded in the clean white kerchief, there a young man with a fair young creature whose wreathed bonnet and snowy veil proclaimed her a newly made bride – and there a decrepit old woman, in the neat tho' rusty black that told of her widowhood.

Not venturing to participate in the communion celebrated that Sunday, he retreated to the gallery, from which he observed one "young and beautiful; her dress was neat… her whole carriage and appearance were so heavenly and so becoming, that when she had received… the sacrament," and retired from the church, his mind was led "into a train

---

[6] *Gospel Messenger*, Feb. 28, 1829.

From Tavern

of serious and melancholy meditations." Though perhaps allowance should be made for the over-heated imagination of a future poet-bishop, his next words reflect the pious gloom of the period.

> Who was she? What was she? Was she blest in life, or was her only pleasure, that, which I had just seen her partake of? [Was she not] soon destined for the grave, and must the grave-worm riot on that lovely cheek?"[7]

In the frequency of the early death of earthly beauty and the inevitable grave, Resignation was a great virtue, particularly for women.

And so was Temperance. That women suffered much from the effects of men's intemperance needs no explanation. Organization to promote temperance became an empowering engine for women's rights. Selection of a symbol of Temperance carried with it an undertone of meaning for women that must rule St. Margaret of Scotland out of any analysis.[8]

The portrayal of the Institution of the Holy Supper was appropriately placed on the distaff side of the church. On the spear side, under the figures of the male apostles with their javelins and staves, were memorials to leading men of the founding of the parish, William Bostwick, Hackaliah Burt, and wardens like Levi Johnson. The commemorated founders of the congregation were men, even though their wives' names are in the windows too. The legal business of the

---

[7] Excerpts [June 23, 1835] from the unpublished diaries of the Rt. Rev. Arthur Cleveland Coxe (1818-96), Second Bishop of Western New York. [Courtesy of Cynthia MacFarland.]

[8] Although St. Margaret *is* credited with civilizing her husband, rude Malcolm.

parish, recorded in the Vestry Minute book of the first seventy years, was all conducted by men. But participating in communion was an activity in which women predominated. Communion was an option which most men passed up.

William H. Seward, a prominent member of the church, married into a family that was a pillar of the parish, served as a vestryman and delegate to Diocesan Convention from 1827 onward, but he was not baptized in the Episcopal Church nor became a communicant until 1837, two years after his wife was admitted to the sacrament..

Men were apparently reluctant to put themselves forward as pious, as holy enough to approach the Table. When church writers like John Rudd kept stressing the special obligation of communicants to 'set an example' in benevolent contributions, it gave pause to a businessman who handled large sums.[9] Women could be benevolent out of their household pin money, or at the end of life in their bequests. Then too, men of the world could be frightened off by admonitions such as the one published in 1875 by Bishop E. B. Tuttle in his Lenten Pastoral:

> Communicants are subject to discipline for immoral conduct…and should avoid public balls, and all places of amusement leading to temptation to break their baptismal vows, and to bring a scandal upon the Church.[10]

Thus by no means was everyone who attended service in the church a communicant. In 1826 only thirty-five of the congregation were communicants. Twenty-five years later that number had grown to one

---

[9] *Gospel Messenger*, Feb. 21, 1829.
[10] Found in Brainard's scrapbook.

hundred and eighty, and in the heady prosperous days in which Dr. Brainard and the vestry planned to build a larger new church, there were less than three hundred communicants. Lots of people came to services, which were mostly Morning Prayer. Communion was observed once a month until the 1890's. On Easter Day 1866 there was a "large congregation" at the ten thirty service, but of the four hundred or more the church could hold, only one hundred and seventy-five stayed for communion.[11]

The communicants of that time were predominantly women. To become a communicant one had to be confirmed or 'ready and desirous' for the same. The clear evidence for a female majority lies in the record of confirmations. From 1826 to 1861 females accounted for 76% of those confirmed. In the same period 80% of those actually registered as communicants at St. Peter's were women.[12]

Of course the daily and weekly work of the parish was done by women. The Vestry, dealing with corporate matters, met on demand. Sometimes there were only two vestry meetings in a whole year. In those days men sold the pews and passed the plate. Women did much of the rest.

Jefferson County author Marietta Holley captured the reality of post-Civil War church life in her depiction of Methodist struggles. The ladies of the fictitious Samantha Allen's church society had been scraping and

---

[11] At the consecration of the first stone church on Monday, August 4, 1833, Frances Seward noted that "the church was filled principally with women." FMS to WHS, August 5, 1833.

[12] Parish Register No. 1. In Advent of 1869, the rector of St. John's, Cohoes, New York, hectored his communicants with a printed letter, identifying them by name. Dr. Brainard saved a copy. Seventy-six percent of the registered communicants in that parish were women.

papering the walls and ceiling of their Meeting House, standing on barrels to do their task, when Samantha's husband Josiah Allen took upon himself to explain why women could not be seated in the General Conference or allowed to mount the "rostrum" at sessions. Josiah assured her,

> that in any modest, unpretendin' way the Methodist Church wuz willin' to accept wimmen's work. It wasn't against the Discipline. And that is why that wimmen have all through the ages been allowed to do most all the hard work in the church – such as raisin' money for church work – earnin' money in all sorts of ways to carry on with the different kinds of charity connected with it – teachin' the children, nursin' the sick, carryin' on hospital work. But, this is far, far different from getttin' up on a rostrum, or tryin' to set on a Conference.[13]

Glimpses of the actual activity of the women of St. Peter's appear in the record. Women were the teachers of the four hundred Sunday School children who marched through the Easter services of 1880 to get a card and candy. During much of the nineteenth century women were the organists and the singers. In 1841 they bought the oil for the lamps for light for winter services. In 1844 they contributed to the parsonage enlargement. In 1863 they provided a more comfortable cushion at the altar rail. In 1874 they made up the Easter flowers in small bunches for the sick. In 1875, the Cook sisters, Melita Chedell, Celuta Cook, Clarissa Hiser, and her daughter, Maria C. Hiser, gave the solid silver chalices, flagon and footed paten still in use today. At the 1870

---

[13] Marietta Holley, *Samantha Among the Brethren*, (New York, 1891), 254.

dedicatory banquet for the new church, a meal of "great taste and liberality" was served by the ladies in the chapel building.[14]

The ladies of 1870 were known as "the Sisterhood," which met on Friday evenings. In 1878 they asked to form a 'Society to complete the chapel.' In 1892 we hear of "St. Peter's Guild." After 1894 there is reference to a "Women's Auxiliary." While the last undoubtedly had a missionary task as well, much of the women's assistance was in working and giving for the furnishings of the church and the enlargement of its facilities.

THE SEWING SCHOOL

In the successful time after the new church was completed in 1870 and its adjoining 'chapel' was then available for broader use, one of the most interesting examples of women's activity was the "Sewing School."

It resembled in format other Sewing Schools like that of Grace Church, Brooklyn Heights. The Annual Report for the "Fifth Year" of this activity in the Brooklyn parish makes plain the intent of that school and provides a "metropolitan" contrast with the Auburn effort.

> This humble and useful Charity would report that it pursued its quiet work on each Saturday morning from November 1869 to May 1870; having in attendance about 100 scholars, under the charge of Miss Sophie T. Sherman, Superintendent, and a score of teachers. Those having the work in charge have borne the expense of the Charity. The children, most of them very poor, are generally warmly attached to the

---

[14] Newspaper report from October 1870.

school and their teachers and show an encouraging degree of improvement. They have made up and received as gifts over 100 garments for their own use. Besides the useful instruction in sewing, it is believed that much good must come from the quiet influences of association with Christian ladies, and of conversation and music, as well as from the regular visits and frequent remarks of the Rector. This useful and comparatively inexpensive Charity might doubtless be enlarged, had it more teachers. The Superintendent and teachers would welcome visits to the school from members of the Parish; and they invite the offer of service from those willing to serve Christ and His poor, through the agency of this Charity. ...November 11, 1870.[15]

St. Peter's "Sewing School" was initiated in 1870, and for almost thirty years was under the administration of Angelica Van Renssalaer Hulbert.[16] The purpose of the school was to show girls how to sew. In the first twenty-five years of its existence the school enrolled nearly 6,000 children from "every church and nationality in Auburn."[17] The girls progressively learned to do more difficult tasks. The classes began at two o'clock on Saturday afternoons and were held for twelve weeks from January to late March. Every year on the last day of the term Dr. Brainard spoke to the children at the crowded closing festivities, where augmented numbers of part-time pupils and their friends would show up for the treat. In the early days prizes of thimbles, pocketbooks, or

---

[15] From a circular carefully preserved by Dr. Brainard in a bound volume of ephemera.
[16] Mrs. Hulbert, the widow of John P. Hulbert, died in December of 1900, at her home at 16 Fort Street, across from the church. She was the daughter-in-law of Caroline Dill, of the "Mount House."
[17] Details derived from clippings in Dr. Brainard's Journal.

From Tavern

handkerchiefs were awarded for excellence in 'buttonhole.' As the girls marched out of the chapel they were given a "bag of cake and an orange." The usual peak enrollment was about 200 girls, who worked on 750 yards of donated cloth, pieced 325 quilt blocks for the Missionary Box, and made for themselves about 360 garments. These numbers remained roughly the same for the time of Mrs. Hulbert's presidency. Each year twenty-five or more teachers and cutters assisted with the instruction. The first Secretary of the school was Carrie Moore, 51 Clark St., and later, the Secretary was Mary Moxley, wife of Robert, a moulder, 12 Church St.

The "Sewing School Hymn" sung in the early days, explains the routine. It was sung to the tune of *Marching Through Georgia*.

> I hear the clock just striking two,
> 'Tis time now to begin.
> From everywhere in Auburn fair
> The girls come flocking in:
> What a busy group we are
> When once we are within,
> While we are singing and sewing.
>
> CHORUS:
> Hurrah! Hurrah! To sewing school we'll go.
> Hurrah! Hurrah! 'Tis there we learn to sew.
> 'Tis there we learn the stitches,
> That each little girl should know
> While we are singing and sewing.

First the overhanding
Is the work we learn to do,
Then to gather, hem and fell
With stitches straight and true;
Then at last we learn to make
A button-hole, can you?
While we are singing and sewing.

CHORUS: Hurrah, etc.

And when, old ladies by the fire
We sit and watch the flames.
And hear the children laugh and sing
At all their merry games,
We'll say, you ought to hear the songs
We sang once to our dames.

In 1899, the school, to which Dr. Brainard referred fondly as "my industrial school," changed administration. After twenty-nine years the eighty-three year old Mrs. Hulbert retired, and the new president was Mrs. William P. Beardsley, of 102 South Street, whose husband was an officer of the Ohio Tool Company and the hereditary treasurer of the Oswego Starch Company. The new Secretary of the school was Josephine Clapp of 208 Genesee St, whose father was the president of Clapp Manufacturing.

Mary Beardsley introduced new measures, modeled after the "Platt Institute" of New York, with heavy emphasis on consistent attendance and uniform accomplishment. It was designated a "marked improvement," a graded system of twenty-four stages, starting with running stitch and leading up to embroidery, a process by which, it was stated, "the children learn they have come here to sew, not to get a garment." Involving twenty-seven teachers, the new system produced fewer quilt blocks for the Missionary Box, only about a hundred, but at the close of the term every girl was given enough flannel to make her own skirt at home. The practical prizes awarded for perfect attendance were work bags, needle cases and pin cushions. And at the end of the annual graduation exercise every girl got the traditional package of cake and an orange.

Out of 207 girls registered in 1900, there were thirty-seven prize-winning young ladies, fifteen with German surnames, five Irish, and seventeen others. By 1903, of the forty-three prize recipients, eight were German, and seven were Irish.

The Reverend John Brainard

Chapter 9

THE BRAINARD ERA: 1863 – 1906
WAR LEADS ON TO THE GILDED AGE

The era in which John Brainard served as Rector of St. Peter's marked not only the longest ministry in the parish's existence by any clergyman but also was the most significant period in the history of the parish. The span of years from 1863 to 1906 saw postwar boom and prosperity, the growth of Auburn's population and industry, the erection of a much larger St. Peter's, the triumph of the Spanish-American War, the passing of Queen Victoria, and the assassination of President McKinley. In this time the old Diocese of Western New York was divided, a new Diocese of Central New York was created and a bishop from Boston, Frederic Dan Huntington, fostered churches in every hamlet from the St. Lawrence to the Susquehanna. John Brainard guided his parish in the developing times, and strengthened the hand of the overseer from Massachusetts with counsel and advice.

John Brainard was born June 4, 1830 in Hartford, Connecticut to Hezekiah and Rebecca (Morgan) Brainard. He received a Bachelor of Arts degree from Trinity College in 1851 and the customary Master of Arts in 1854. He was ordained a deacon in the Protestant Episcopal Church by Bishops Brownell and Williams[1] on December 18, 1853. He served a two-year apprenticeship as assistant at Grace Church, Baltimore, Maryland, under the supervision of the rector, the Rev.

---

[1] Bishop Williams exhorted him in the sermon that day to serve faithfully, "until you reach the rest and quiet of the grave."

Arthur Cleveland Coxe, and was made priest on May 15, 1856, having been called to the parish of St. James', Birmingham, Connecticut.

On December 11, 1861 he married Antoinette Judson, the daughter of Donald Judson, a jurist and Connecticut state senator. The new priest's ministry of seven years at Birmingham, Connecticut, was distinguished by increased attendance at church, large confirmation classes, and a growing reputation as a guest preacher. In Connecticut he was a member of the National Guard but was not called to active service even as the Civil War grew increasingly serious.

Reverend John Brainard during the Civil War

In September of 1863, as the war continued in the South and West, he was invited to visit Auburn as a candidate for the position of rector. In late October he said goodbye to his parishioners and friends in Connecticut and accepted the call of St. Peter's vestry. Certainly he was recommended to the post by Arthur Cleveland Coxe. Arriving in Auburn by train in early November of 1863, he was accompanied by his very pregnant wife[2] and her widowed mother, Mrs. P. M. Judson.

On the last leg of that train journey, the Brainard family were accompanied by their new parishioner, the Secretary of State of the United States of America, the Hon. William H. Seward, who greeted his rector-to-be and welcomed the newcomers to Auburn.[3] That first acquaintance with the distinguished statesman was a foretaste of things to come.

They were met at the Auburn station by an enthusiastic group of men, "more men at one time," remarked Brainard later, "than I seldom saw again, except at Easter services." Among them was General John H. Chedell, whose influence and promised support was a strong factor in convincing the young man from Connecticut to choose Auburn for a successful ministry. An additional reason for his choice was the certainty that his former rector in Baltimore, Arthur Cleveland Coxe, would be elected as the next bishop of Western New York. Coxe had been the preferred choice for the responsibility for years and indeed, without formal nomination, was elected on August 19, 1864, to succeed the failing Bishop DeLancey.

---

[2] Their son John Morgan Brainard was born on December 21, 1863.

[3] "At election time in 1863, Seward was in Auburn, called there by the illness of William Henry, Jr." Glyndon G. Van Deusen, *William H. Seward*, (New York: Oxford, 1967), 392.

Mr. Brainard inherited a fine stone church which had been expanded to twice its original size. The finances seemed somewhat problematic and the church had had a succession of short ministries. Of three rectors in the last ten years, one had given up due to poor health, one had left after two years for a chaplaincy in the Army, and one had died suddenly after a year in office. Yet the parish had great potential and was very promising for a pastor who would stay for the right period of parochial work and responsible shepherding.

Soon John Brainard's weekly journal entries reported large congregations, filling up the stone church's one hundred and twelve pews below and twenty-five in the gallery. On Thanksgiving Day 1864, the parish observed a relic of the old Donation Day for the minister, and the rector, noting "this is a very pleasing result," received a purse of $238.50 for himself plus "from N. Fitch, $25 for the poor." He was continually impressed by the large crowds at funerals and at the Sunday services.

On January 8, 1865, the pleased pastor recorded, "This has been one of the happiest days of my life. Rt. Rev. Dr. Coxe held a visitation in this parish. At 9 AM he went to the prison, where after prayers by Mr. Russell, he preached. At 10 ½ service began in church...After the sermon I presented 54 candidates for confirmation...The day has been fine, the church crowded. I have enjoyed the day beyond account."

The poetical and handsome Arthur Cleveland Coxe had just been consecrated as a bishop four days before, and the first exercise of his episcopal office was granted to the growing parish of his former assistant. In May Bishop Coxe returned to Auburn for a second confirmation, this time for a group of twenty-six. That made a total for the year of eighty confirmands, a bounty indeed.[4]

But much of 1865 was destined to be a time of sorrow. Young John Morgan Brainard almost died of the croup. In April the funeral of Bishop William H. DeLancey took place in Geneva. And on the Saturday before Easter came the terrible news that President Lincoln was dead and that William H. Seward and his sons had been nearly killed by another of the assassins.[5] At St. Peter's on the day of President Lincoln's funeral, additional mourning draperies were added to the ones already hung for Bishop Delancey, and there was the first of many civic outpourings of grief in which St. Peter's church became the location for Auburn's expression of emotion. The crowds continued through the Sunday after Easter, only to return a few months later in June on the occasion of the death of Mrs. Seward who had been brought low by stress over the attack upon her husband and their sons. A great throng gathered for her funeral in Auburn and filled St. Peter's as an evidence of their regard for the stricken statesman.

Christmas of 1865 brings the first mention of the successful observance of a "Christmas Eve" service in a packed church. And on the following Christmas Day the church began an annual custom, a practice which lasted till the end of Brainard's life, the charity of providing the

---

[4] Of the fifty-four confirmed in January, thirty made their communion on February 5th, and of the twenty-six added in May, seventeen came to communion on May 7th.

[5] "Easter Even. We received the startling intelligence this day that the President of the United States had been assassinated and that Secretary Seward & sons were at the point of death from the attacks of murderers. The whole community are in tears." Brainard's Journal, April 15, 1865.

Christmas Dinner at the Orphan Asylum, completed by an address by the rector to the recipients.

The succeeding years were marked by increasing congregations and large classes to be confirmed. It became more and more evident that the church needed to be enlarged to accommodate the growing numbers of worshippers. More income was also needed. At a time when offerings at services were taken only for special purposes, the principal way the parish gained income was by allowing supporters to bid on a pew of their choice and then annually thereafter assessing a rental based on a percentage of the resulting valuation. Forty added pews were judged to increase the income base by a major fraction.

The beginning of John Brainard's tenure affords a good point at which to take notice of the social composition of the parish. An analysis of the baptisms in 1865 shows that the economic background of the families involved was approximately 25% that of employers and professionals, 40% from the merchant class, and 35% from those who worked at shops or farms. In September the first vestryman whose death was memorialized in the minutes of the parish was senior Warden Levi Johnson, co-owner of a bookstore and stationery business.

In January of 1866 the vestry formed a committee to consider another expansion of the church. The first plan was to add to the length of the sides to gain 38 pews at a cost of $3800.

At the same time the parish grew more confident, raised the rector's salary and increased the percentage tax on the existing pews. There was a large number of worshippers at the Easter services of whom 175 came to communion. In September Bishop Coxe confirmed another fifty people. In 1866 water and sewer services were connected to the rectory for the first time.

Large congregations in Lent of 1867 convinced the vestry that a more serious scheme of church enlargement was needed. Rough plans drawn by George Casey, a vestryman and contractor, contemplated an expenditure of fifteen to twenty thousand dollars, and the vestry determined to get an architect to perfect the project.

In early 1868 the firm of Draper and Dudley was selected as architects for a new church which would incorporate part of the existing structure, the chancel end to the north and the transepts, but which would provide a wider and longer nave. The old nave would be taken down and reassembled as a chapel, slightly to the side and rear of the north end of the old church. In this way the congregation would not be required to worship for long in borrowed premises.

In March 1868 Mr. Brainard recorded that "during the week our organ has been taken down and packed up in view of the speedy enlargement and reconstruction of the church." On March 29th the final service in the old church was held. "The church was densely packed…I preached an historical sermon of great length which was listened to with unflagging attention. This closes up religious services in Old St. Peter's Church, Auburn."[6]

---

[6] The sermon and other historical materials were published in an eighty page booklet, *The History of St. Peter's Church, Auburn, N.Y., A Sermon Preached on Sunday Evening, March 29, 1868, Being the Last Occasion of Worship in the Old Church Previous to its Reconstruction*, by Rev. John Brainard, M.A., Rector. Auburn: Printed by Dennis Brothers, No. 4 Mechanic Street, 1868.

Weekday services were held for a time in Central Presbyterian Church, and on Sundays the parish worshipped in the Court House. Part of the pressure for accommodation was relieved by the initiation of a new Episcopal congregation in the "Eastern District" of the city, a group known as St. John's which met in a schoolhouse on Fulton Street and which was also served by Brainard. At Easter there were three hundred and fifty-five in attendance at the Court House and the Fulton Street schoolhouse was "crowded." The busy rector closed the day by noting, "I have done a heavy days work…Church matters are prospering considerably in Auburn."

Central Presbyterian was used for the bishop's visitation in April, but by fall of 1868 the reconstructed chapel had been readied at St. Peter's. On All Saint's day the congregation returned to its own building whose smaller accommodation was compensated for by the enthusiasm about St. John's parish. But since the newer congregation had no construction expenses as yet, the vestry decided to ask its members who had transferred from St. Peter's to continue to honor their subscriptions to St. Peter's building fund.

The winter of 1868-1869 was an active time for the Episcopalians of central New York. A primary convention for the new Diocese of Central New York was held in Utica. It elected a candidate for bishop who suddenly chose not to accept the post. A second convention was called for January, and Frederic Dan Huntington of Boston was elected. Mr. Brainard, as befitted the rector of one of the larger parishes, presided briefly at the organizing session of the convention. He was elected to the Standing Committee of the new diocese, a capacity in which he served for the entire time of Bishop Huntington's episcopate.

While the new church building was still under construction in 1869, John Brainard's talents were duly recognized by the vestry of St. Paul's Church, New Haven, Connecticut. The prominent parish sent delegates to Auburn and a call was extended to him in April to become their new rector. While he wrote in his journal, "I should love to go," the vestry of St. Peter's was not about to part with their popular and successful rector, especially in the middle of the construction and financing of a major new edifice. The alarmed board dispatched to him a motion of support, composed by General Chedell, in which they emphasized that he had their united respect and confidence and love, and expressed the hope "that nothing may occur so long as his life shall be spared to induce him to resign." The following July they increased his salary from sixteen hundred to two thousand dollars a year and invited him to take an annual vacation of six weeks.

In a double stroke of tragedy, John Brainard's newborn son perished at the end of that summer and his wife Antoinette, succumbing to tuberculosis at thirty-two, died a month later. "This morning my dear child Edward Sheldon Brainard was called home to his heavenly rest…A child safe, eternally safe, is a blessing for which I thank Almighty God."[August 27, 1869] "Administered Holy Communion to my dear wife, who is rapidly failing in health and strength."[September 5, 1869] "This day my dear wife entered into Everlasting rest." [October 1, 1869] Child and mother were both interred in Hartford. A saddened John Brainard returned to his work in Auburn.

Apparently the work and resources for the new church began to lag somewhat. In the summer of 1869 the vestry mortgaged the rectory for ten thousand dollars and made General Chedell a member of the building committee, empowered to employ "as large a force…as shall be deemed expedient." Pressure was applied to finish the project.

FROM TAVERN

As one of the last major construction decisions the vestry had been persuaded to have the elaborate frame of the large round window in the south wall of the church fabricated of Caen stone rather than the less expensive medium of wood. As the building neared completion, young William Edward Chedell, with his certain death approaching, sent five hundred dollars, part to be used for the purchase of a stone baptismal font to be inscribed with his name. The vestry accepted the gift and resolved that the "large wheel window" should be named for him and considered "his" window.

On Easter Day, April 17, 1870, the congregation of St. Peter's Church met for the first time in the much larger new building. "We assembled within our new church this morning, glad and thankful for the privilege of keeping the feast within its walls. There was a very large congregation." The following day, Easter Monday, the customary annual parish meeting took place, with "large attendance and harmonious results."

On October 10, 1870 the vestry prepared the "Instrument of Donation" and on St. Luke's Day, October 18th, St. Peter's reconstructed and greatly enlarged church was consecrated by Bishop Frederic Dan Huntington, assisted by Bishop Arthur Cleveland Coxe of Western New York. The proud rector, now Doctor Brainard,[7] recorded that the "exhilarating…delightful" ceremonies were attended by a large number of clergy and an immense throng of laity.

The parish was now well equipped with space for worship. To what use was the "chapel," the building to the side of the main church, to be put?

---

[7] John Brainard was awarded the degree of Doctor of Divinity by Trinity College in July 1870.

It was available on Sundays to accommodate the Sunday School which had met for long in the additions to the rear of the rectory. But such a large, "neutral," space as the chapel provided now found more use. In the fall of 1870, leading up to Christmas, there is the first mention of "the Sisterhood." This group had likely prepared the dinner served in the chapel to the guests at the October 18th dedication of the church. Meetings of the Sisterhood were held on Fridays that November and early December. A Christmas tree was featured at the Christmas Eve service and there was a "grand congregation" on Christmas Day in 1870.

St. George's Day, April 23, 1871, marked the beginning of the annual gathering at St. Peter's of the St. George's Society, whose visitations continued throughout the rest of the century. This charitable fraternity was supported by men of English origin. The antecedents of the organization appear both in New York and in Toronto.[8] Dr. Brainard was usually joined in these anglophile celebrations by the rectors of other area churches.

On October 15, 1871, a Sunday, Dr. Brainard, who had just returned from Baltimore, recorded his themes for the day. "In the morning I made the late Chicago disaster my subject.[9] At night gave an account of the General Convention."

Precisely one year later there came a day both welcome and sad. The vestry met the evening of October 14, 1872, the day of Governor Seward's funeral, to consider a munificent proposal by General Chedell.

---

[8] The New York chapter of the organization cited Bishop Benjamin Moore (1748-1816) as its founder and had as its motto, "Let memory be our only boast and shame our only fear."

[9] The Chicago Fire.

From Tavern

In a letter to the vestry the general noted that while the base portion of the tower had been constructed, the bell tower and spire of the church were as yet incomplete. About thirty thousand dollars had been raised and spent for the building fund, and another fifteen to eighteen thousand had been borrowed. Ten thousand of that had been obtained by a mortgage on the rectory. There was additionally about six thousand in floating debt. The wealthy patron stated that he would like to see the church completed but that he thought it unlikely with such debts outstanding.

His magnanimous offer to the parish followed. If the vestry would promise to raise the funds necessary to pay off the six thousand dollars in floating debt, he would finish the tower and spire in stone, at his own expense.

The vestry gratefully accepted the challenge, and the work began to complete the tower and to gain subscriptions to pay off the unsecured debt. In the next several years the vestry worked successfully to deal with delinquencies in pew rents and in debt reduction. After such a flurry of activity and decisions in the preceding years, few vestry meetings were now necessary, only two in 1873 and merely one in 1874.

The formal memorial observance by the State of New York to mark the passing of William H. Seward took place in Albany April 18, 1873. The printed program called for Bishop A. C. Coxe to give the blessing. Dr. Brainard attended as an honored guest and became a participant. "In Albany at memorial services for Hon. W. H. Seward. It was a very impressive service. The address by Mr. Charles Francis Adams was very fine.... I pronounced the benediction."

Mrs. John Chedell, Melita Cook, died in March of 1874. The following Sunday, March 15, 1874, Dr. Brainard's sermon "alluded to the death of President Fillmore, Charles Sumner, and Mrs. Chedell." Enos Thompson Throop, former Governor of New York, died in November 1874 at the age of ninety. His funeral was held in the church on November 4th.

Easter of 1875 saw the presentation of "a new and splendid communion service of solid silver," two chalices, a footed paten, and a large flagon. The paten was given by Ruth Newell Smith in memory of Ezra Powell Smith, MD. One chalice was the gift of Miss Maria Cook Hiser in memory of her mother Clarissa Cook Hiser. The second chalice was donated by Miss Hiser and her aunt Miss Celuta Cook in memory of General Chedell's widow, their aunt and sister Melita Cook Chedell. The large flagon, given by Miss Hiser, was given in the memory of the former rector and patriotic chaplain, Charles H. Platt, but additionally inscribed "Rev. John Brainard, D.D., Rector."

Nor were the dedications of the year complete. In April the vestry was invited to approve, as a replacement for the single bell, the installation of a chime of bells in the finished tower. The ten bells were to be paid for by private subscription and the work to be supervised by Mr. Edward Davis. When installed, two of the bells were the gift of the St. George's Society and the Salem Town Commandery of the Knights Templar. Another was in memory of Mr. Cyrus Dennis, a partner with David M. Osborne in the manufacture of agricultural machinery. The rest were paid for by private donations from church members and a gentleman from the Universalist church. Dedicated on Sunday the Fourth of July in 1875, the bells were rung to accompany Dr. Brainard's memorial sermon for General Chedell.

From Tavern

For the magnificent patron, bereft of wife and children, had relinquished his earthly life at the end of June 1875. "Attended funeral of my dear friend and parishioner," wrote Dr. Brainard on the twenty-second of June.

The vestry gave appropriate expression to the parish's loss.

> Resolved, that in the death of General Chedell this Church has lost one of its most earnest and exemplary members, and our vestry its wisest and most valued advisor. Attached strongly to the service of the Episcopal Church of which he was for so many years a member, to this Church in particular he was ever warmly devoted. It stands today a monument to his munificent liberality. He accepted towards it, and towards the community generally, the responsibility which his ability, his social position and large wealth imposed. He recognized that he was the steward of his Master, and those who knew him best will testify, how well and how willingly he fulfilled those duties.
>
> Resolved, that as a citizen, few if any will remember when he was not a leading man in this community. One of its oldest citizens, he has at all times stood at the forefront in all enterprises connected with the development of our city. His large practical common sense, his earnestness and public spirit always and everywhere commanded respect. He was the peer of the strongest. The place he vacates will not be filled by any one man. Such men are not duplicated, and it behooves us each to take up a portion of the burden he has laid down, and endeavor to carry it as well as we may.

On July 9, 1875 the vestry was apprised of the further generosity of General Chedell and of the responsibilities he had laid upon them. By the fifteenth clause of his will he donated an additional ten thousand dollars to St. Peter's to pay off the mortgage on the rectory. He turned over to St. Peter's vestry the deed to the lot he had designated for St. John's Church, requiring them to hold the property until St. John's should actually build upon it. As an inducement to the new parish he gave in trust to St. Peter's vestry the sum of ten thousand dollars which should go toward the cost of St. John's church building. St. Peter's was debt free, and its vestry charged to oversee their daughter parish in its anticipated response to the generosity of the great benefactor.

The year 1876 began in happy fashion. On January 2 Dr. Brainard wrote that the day was so warm that the church doors were opened. "Mrs. Knight gave me a little bunch of violets picked in their garden this morning." Twenty-two children were given a silver dollar each for saying their catechism perfectly. "Today I announced to the congregation that I had paid off the entire indebtedness of the Church."

On Palm Sunday Bishop Huntington confirmed forty-seven successful catechumens. After Easter the rector traveled to New York with his bride-to-be and on May 11th was married in St. Thomas' Church by his cousin the Rev. William H. Morgan. After seven years as a widower, John Brainard found a wife and companion in Cornelia Fatzinger, the widow of Levi Fatzinger, Waterloo's woolen manufacturer. After a honeymoon in Boston the newlyweds returned to Auburn on May 19th. The marriage served to augment Dr. Brainard's affinity for Waterloo. For many years he traveled to the neighboring village every Ash Wednesday evening to preach for his good friend the Rev. William Doty, rector of St. Paul's.

FROM TAVERN

On Sunday, July 2, 1876, the parish held a Centenary Service to mark the one hundredth anniversary of the United States of America, an institution only twenty-nine years older than St. Peter's itself.

Eighteen seventy-six marked the first election to the vestry of David Munson Osborne. The great industrialist took an active role in regulating the income of the parish and in finishing the interior arrangement of the church. As the implications of General Chedell's complicated will were slowly worked out, the manufacturer's presence and support was truly needed.

As the members of St. John's gathered their strength gradually for the construction of a church on the donated lot at the corner of East Genesee and Fulton, their thoughts gravitated to the ten thousand dollars held in trust by St. Peter's vestry. In 1877 the vestry of St. John's went to court to press St. Peter's to construe that the interest from the trust should be turned over to St. John's to sustain the current expense of their worship services. Somehow this was worked out and the court actions relieved St. Peter's trustees of private decision.

Meanwhile, even though there were now two Episcopal churches in the city, St. Peter's grew apace. The confirmation class in 1877 numbered sixty.

An analysis of the baptisms in 1875 offers insight into the nature of the growing membership of St. Peter's. Of the thirty-nine baptisms performed by Dr. Brainard in 1875, an impressive three-quarters were of adults or children of parents from the socio-economic class of employees and workers. Ten percent were from the upper 'professional' group and fifteen percent came from the middle ranks of merchants and shop owners. These proportions held for the baptisms ten years later in 1885, again with ten percent from the professional category, twenty-five percent from the merchant and shop owner ranks, and over half, as far as can be determined, from the families of workers and employees.

In 1877, "twilight services" of Evening Prayer at six or six-thirty on Sunday, in the summer months from June to the end of September, were substituted for the customary prayers at three in the afternoon. Working class people, especially those in domestic service, could find it possible to attend service late on Sunday, when all their tasks were accomplished and they could take time off. And a later hour did not conflict with working people's Sunday amusements.

In a parallel development the year 1878 brought the first mention of quarterly collections for parish expenses. Pew rents had been payable in quarterly installments for some time, but those rents came only from the smaller number of well-established persons who paid whether they were in church or not. Increased numbers at services gave an opportunity to pass the offering plate and open the purses of ordinary folk who were paid weekly in cash.

On Friday June 14, 1878, Dr. Brainard met in the chapel with a number of ladies to consider the establishment of a "society to complete the chapel." The heating arrangement for the chapel at that time remains a mystery, but it is certain that like the church, the auxiliary building was served by neither water nor sewer nor the amenities associated with them. "Completion" certainly meant more than decorations. On All Saints' Day there was the annual meeting of "St. Peter's Sisterhood."

The terrible winter in early 1879 emphasized the importance of dependable heating, when a blinding snowstorm lasted for over four days. And the buildings needed to be more accommodating as their use increased. That April David Osborne moved that the vestry consider introducing steam and water into the church and chapel, with proper sewerage. As the "program" of the parish grew, chiefly at the initiative of the women, the desire for more convenient arrangements developed.

The chapel must have been filled with young warm humanity on important Sundays, as Dr. Brainard's seventeen years of dependable ministry and Auburn's growing population met in a crescendo of popularity. On Easter Day in 1880 no less than four hundred Sunday school children swelled the crowd and processed through the church to receive their Easter candy and card at the hands of the beaming rector.

The Fourth of July in 1880 fell on a Sunday. St. Peter's was the host church for an observance of the 104th Anniversary of the nation. "Nearly all the clergy of the city and the Mayor present," noted the rector.

The old order was passing. That was illustrated in the death of William Allen in the first month of 1881. This successful lawyer had been born in 1817 in the Saratoga area and in Auburn had developed a law practice described in the fulsome memorial written by the vestry as "large, lucrative, and eminently successful." Associated with a legal firm that over time included some of the most prominent lawyers in Auburn, he had been elected to the vestry of St. Peter's for nineteen successive years. In July 1881 President Garfield was shot, and upon his death in September the memorial service in St. Peter's was "very largely attended by a deeply affected multitude."

More deaths continued in 1882. At fifty-one Edward H. Groot, a successful businessman who had been a vestryman for sixteen years, passed away. Ten years before he had chaired the committee to decorate the church for Seward's funeral and married Miss Meachem, one of the young ladies who assisted at the arrangements. The parish also learned that their former rector, the energetic Mr. Ayrault, had died in Geneva.

In May of 1883 David M. Osborne moved that the vestry proceed with plans to extend the chancel, enlarge the vestry room [the present sacristy], and construct an organ chamber on the east side of the church. He accepted membership on the committee to carry out the plans. In this matter and in the issue of the heat and water in the previous years, it is clear, knowing what we do of church leadership practices at the time, that his initiation and endorsement of the plans implied that he not only favored the proposal strongly but was indicating that he would contribute significantly toward the costs.

By June 1883 the vestry was ready to go ahead with the plans. As 1884 progressed funds were borrowed to finish the chancel work and to proceed with the procurement of "a system of steam heat and apparatus with all needed improvements as called for." The chancel enlargement extended a portion thirty-two feet wide northward by an additional twenty-six feet, and added a robing room and an organ chamber. On March 2nd, 1884 the "new" church with its extended chancel was again opened for service. The observance on Thanksgiving Day, wrote the rector, had a "congregation larger than I have ever known."

Dr. Brainard had been paying the bills and costs of part of the work, so that in 1885 the vestry repaid him with their note for four thousand dollars. As such a promissory note bore a favorable rate of interest, the practice testifies to the depth of Brainard's resources and to the freedom granted to him in procurement of services.

From Tavern

Mrs. Judson, the mother of Dr. Brainard's first wife, died in May of 1885. The rector's good friend, the Rev. Charles Hawley, minister of the First Presbyterian Church, went to his reward in November of that year.

On the Sunday before Easter of 1886 the rector recorded that "the church was elegantly decorated with huge palm branches sent from the Bahama Islands by the Hon. D. M. Osborne." Unfortunately the trip to recover his health was of no avail to the prominent industrialist and at the age of sixty-four on July 6, 1886, Mr. Osborne passed away at his Auburn home.

The vestry met the next day to formulate a memorial for their fellow churchman.

> He was the friend and earnest advocate of good causes and beneficent enterprises, and he gave liberally of his substance to promote their advancement. Just, firm, courageous, open-handed and large-hearted, the sway of his great faculties trended always into generous and sympathetic grooves; and so, he was helpful and useful, and his life in manifold ways was a blessing to society.
>
> He was accorded rank among the great manufacturers of Christendom, and the clangor of his machinery, like England's drumbeat, "encircles the globe" and "is heard round the world."
>
> Always the supreme factor in the large circle of his business activities, in social life and public affairs, where divided responsibility and varying opinions incite debate, his

character was not marred by self-assertion nor its noble symmetry blurred by selfishness.

And the memorial further emphasized that "He was faithful and loyal in every relation in life — to this church, to his family, to society, to his country."

In November of 1886 the rector announced to the vestry "that the family of the late David M. Osborne had expressed to him their wish to present an organ to St. Peter's church as a memorial of Mr. Osborne." The vestry moved to authorize any "changes in the chancel necessary for the reception of the organ."

At the same time they voted to arrange the heating system so that the church and the chapel could be heated separately. This seems to provide evidence that use of the chapel was required on more than Sundays.

In March of 1887 the D. M. Osborne Memorial organ was in place, a Hilbourne Roosevelt production, considered a very fine organ of that era. The vestry insured it for four thousand dollars.

The previous arrangement for singers and organ had been in a gallery over the entrance portion of the building. The gallery was entered by a door, still to be seen, which opened from a landing of the tower stairway. The new organ, now located in an organ chamber on the east side of the chancel, had the effect of concentrating the musical aspect of the service in the front, the chancel end, of the church. The old organ, played in a gallery above the main floor, had obviously been pumped by hand. The new organ was pumped by a water engine in the basement below, making use of the water introduced into the north end of the church from the Church Street main. The old organ was given to St. John's Church.

At this point the gallery was removed and the entrance area gained the full height of the nave so that the wheel window could be seen clearly from directly below. The gallery extensions no longer obscured the view over the last west window. The singers were now located in or near the chancel. Dr. Brainard mentions the names of various female soloists who "sang all day" at the multiple services.

The resulting attractions had their effect over Good Friday and Easter of 1887, when the weather was good and the church was filled to its capacity of nearly seven hundred worshippers who were delighted with the powerful new organ and a visible choir. In the middle of June St. Peter's was host to the diocesan convention. The next week, Dr. Brainard, something of an expert in such matters, congratulated the members of the Baptist church across the corner on extinguishing the debt for their new edifice. In 1887 the "twilight services" were continued through the end of October.

The observance of Dr. Brainard's twenty-fifth anniversary as rector was the high point of 1888. That Easter marked the first instance of an "early service" at eight am. An overflow crowd at the later service that day produced five hundred and forty-nine communicants. The eight o'clock service was continued all throughout the summer months. In mid-November the statue of Governor Seward was dedicated in the park on South Street, to the accompaniment of St. Peter's chimes. The rector pronounced the blessing.

The silver anniversary of John Brainard's ministry in Auburn was observed in the week following All Saints' Day with a grand surprise party at the rectory and the production of a special booklet. The principal gift was a tall solid silver pitcher made by Tiffany's which remains today in the parish's possession. The booklet contained accounts of the events, remarks by his close clerical friends, and letters of congratulation from more than fifty persons, with the names of another fifty who had responded with letters. The organizations of the parish were outlined and statistics recounted for the current year.[10]

At the outset of the year 1888 the parish had received a magnificent gift in the form of six sterling silver offering plates. The donor was the Honorable Samuel Blatchford, Associate Justice of the Supreme Court of the United States. Justice Blatchford had risen to prominence, first as clerk to Governor Seward, then as a distinguished attorney and the author of records and summaries of the decisions of the high court. He had lived in Auburn as a young man and in 1847 was elected a vestryman and for six years thereafter.

These elegantly simple plates, intended to be passed by the ushers to every person present at a service, demonstrated a growing emphasis at St. Peter's on the collection of a weekly contribution from individuals. It was becoming evident that a more systematic procedure than pew rents and occasional offerings would be needed to provide a regular and wider base of church support.

Easter of the year 1889 saw fifty communicants at the first service and a packed church at ten thirty. Holy Communion now was observed each Sunday at eight am, and on the first Sunday of the month at noon

---

[10] They are listed in an appendix of the booklet.

when it followed the late service of Morning Prayer. On Christmas Day of 1889 the parish served its 27th annual Christmas dinner to the Cayuga Orphans Asylum.

There seemed little for the vestry to do, the parish possessed three auxiliary organizations for women and a large Sunday School. Only one vestry meeting was necessary in 1889 and again in 1890 to organize its supervisory committees. Miss Celuta Cook, General Chedell's sister-in-law, died in August of 1889, and her estate devolved on Miss Maria Cook Hiser, her niece. The vestry agreed to Miss Hiser's life use of the income from the portion Miss Cook had designated for the parish's eventual endowment.

In 1891 a group from the congregation petitioned the vestry for the establishment of a vested choir. After deliberation the vestry decided that they could not bear the expense of the innovation and that there would also be no place to seat such a choir.[11]

Noah P. Clarke, warden for sixteen years, died in 1892, and the parish lost another prominent businessman and public figure.

Eighteen ninety-three was the centennial of Auburn's founding. On July 2 a service marked by a crowded church was held in observance of that milestone. In October the Wheeler Rifles, Auburn's own militia unit, attended a special service in full uniform, and Dr. Brainard addressed them appropriately. General John N. Knapp, who had played

---

[11] This makes one wonder what all the chancel area _was_ devoted to. It surely held the organ console, prayer desks, clergy seats, some choir seating, lectern, pulpit, altar, bishop's chair and altar rail easily within a space recently extended by twenty-six feet. Was the vestry just resisting change?

such a prominent role in the enlargement of the church in 1860, was the next parish stalwart to pass away.

The Spanish-American War of 1898 called away the Wheeler Rifles for service in the south. On May 8 the rector's "remarks were upon the War and the duty of a Christian man in such times of national trial." On Ascension Day the attendance was unusually good. July 10th saw a "service of Praise and Thanksgiving for naval victories" and August brought a "Thanksgiving service for blessings of Peace."

From 1893 and 1894 there had been a changing understanding of the new realities of Auburn's growing population which influenced the vestry's approach to fund raising. First, the pew selection was no longer to be solemnized by annual auction or bidding. Instead pew renters were merely to contact the sexton and make their selections from his chart. Pew rents, although increased by a whopping twenty-five percent in 1894, continued to bring in about the same actual amount each year, an indication that support for pews had surely stabilized.

In 1893 the vestry moved to initiate a practice of providing quarterly reports of its finances to the congregation, an indication generally that the purse of any reporting body grows thin.[12] In June of 1894 the vestry heard a report on a new system, "a scheme of weekly pledges." The following week Dr. Brainard devoted his sermon to the "pledge system."

In 1895 the first "Treasurer of weekly pledges" was chosen to keep the books on the pledges and to turn over the proceeds regularly to the general treasurer of the vestry, who was already the keeper of the income

---

[12] A major industrial depression struck the nation in early 1893 and continued until 1897.

from the pews. The pew income provided three to four thousand dollars per year, and "pledge" income varied widely from fourteen hundred to nine hundred dollars in any given year. One can see that the stalwart pew "owners" continued to be the main base for income, but that a way was opened for younger and less affluent supporters to do more than make occasional contributions for special requests.

This observation is illuminated by an analysis of the baptisms in 1895. Two-thirds of the baptisms involved families or individuals from the worker and employee level, one-fourth represented the small business and merchant grouping, and only seven percent came from Auburn's wealthier professionals and managers.

And, as a marker of changing practices, 1895 was the occasion of the first instance of the practice of cremation in Dr. Brainard's ministry.

In 1896 and 1897 there were few meetings of the vestry, as the parish ran along in a well-established pattern. The "scheme of weekly pledges" got off to a fair start with annual contributions of approximately fourteen hundred dollars, applied to total parish expenditures of forty-six hundred dollars. The bulk of the annual income continued to be from the pews, roughly thirty-four hundred dollars each year. But the pledged income dropped off by about a hundred dollars in each following year, so that in 1900 the pledges brought in little over nine hundred dollars.

One of the causes of this diminishment of "non-pew" income was the need for subscriptions to repair the tower. By November of 1898 the first major repairs to St. Peter's tower and spire had become unavoidable. A contractor was engaged and in December Mr. W. H. Gorsline submitted a bill for the initial work. The tower was shored up as much as possible and the major work planned for the following spring. From May to September the vestry continued to borrow funds to pay for the work and the final bill came to six thousand two hundred dollars, or one and a half times the annual budget.

Another cause of the reduction in payments to the weekly pledge system was the growing activity of the ladies of the parish who in their "Sisterhood," Guild, and Auxiliary were building up treasuries of their own. It was not that less money was coming in, it was just not going directly to the vestry. Storing up their own treasuries, the ladies were now directly in position to influence the flow of events. In 1900 the vestry moved to consider an enlargement of the vestibule. Previously there seems to have been a wooden storm shed in front of the main entrance. At the same time the men responded to a request to improve the ventilation of the chapel, made stifling by the large numbers of the Sunday School and the deserving youth of the neighborhood.

The most significant example of the influence of the women's funds came in 1903 when Dr. Brainard was able to purchase the Hills property, the house and lot on the very north-east corner of James and Genesee.[13] For this building, which adjoined the church tract and fronted on Genesee Street, the total cost was $8,750. The parish treasurer provided $350 for the down payment, and the ladies furnished the generous sum of $2,400. A six thousand dollar mortgage on the property, held by the trustees of the Presbyterian Seminary, was assumed by the parish, with the guild and the auxiliary paying the

---

[13] Jannat Swain Hills was born in Devonshire in 1823 to sea captain William Swain and his wife Catherine, who emigrated to America when she was seven. She was a devout member of St. Peter's, married William Hills, had ten children and was widowed in 1875. She died July 20, 1902.

service on the debt. Certainly it was these two organizations who advised the vestry to name the house they had purchased, "St. Peter's Church Parish House."

In 1901, the founder of the "Sewing School," Mrs. Angelica Van Renssalaer Hulbert left the parish about nine thousand dollars. Her will specified that only the income from the legacy was to be spent for repairs to the church, and that in any year in which no repairs were made the income was to be paid to the rector. The church already had an unrestricted endowment of about two thousand dollars, as well as a fourteen hundred dollar future interest in the estate of Celuta Cook, of which Miss Hiser was the beneficiary for life.

The year 1901 was the occasion for several memorial services of wide interest. At Evensong on the 27th of January "an immense congregation gathered for a Memorial of Queen Victoria the good." The General Gordon Lodge of the St. George Society, the Sons of St. George, and the Red Rose Lodge (the ladies auxiliary) attended with their flags. The Queen's picture, draped in black, was placed before the altar, and the chimes played "God save the queen." Dr. Brainard remarked upon the fact that due to modern inventions, "the whole world heard it at once." On September 8th the shocking news was telegraphed that there had been an attempt on the life of President McKinley. When the president died a week later yet another memorial service was held in St. Peter's, "crowded to the doors, and all about the church."

That fall the rector attended the General Convention in San Francisco, visiting Salt Lake City and the Grand Canyon on a trip that lasted two months.

Three quarters of a century earlier, Bishop John Henry Hobart had struggled against the threat that protestants might overwhelm the "apostolic" Episcopal Church by co-opting it into the "benevolent empire" of the Bible and Tract Societies. Back then the danger had come from the affinity of Episcopalian evangelicals to their fellows in the reformed churches. In Hobart's time "High Church" carried the meaning of a strong assertion of the apostolic and catholic heritage of the church inherited from the mother country. In 1901 the danger perceived by Bishop Frederic Dan Huntington was from the other side of the Anglican 'via media.' The affirmation of the church's catholic heritage had taken form in ritualistic practices which the old New Englander found fussy, needless, and offensive. That they were "Romish" he found it unnecessary to state. That they were individualistic departures from usage and Prayer Book, he warned.

It was not customary in the Gay Nineties to have candles burning on the altar. "Eucharistic lights" as they were called, were frequently an affectation by young clergy, who in Bishop Huntington's view, were too fond of popish practices. Confronted with the rare practice, the bishop would caustically remark that he "preferred sunshine" or that he could see without extra light. Once the excuse was made to him that candles were needed on a dark day. When the sun came out Bishop Huntington picked up each candlestick and blew out the flame, telling the young minister that "now he could see all right."[14]

Dr. Brainard pasted into his journal the Bishop's pastoral letter of Ash Wednesday, 1901, in which Huntington inveighed against and prohibited some additional practices which twice had irked him so much that he had left the chancel when they were forced upon him.

---

[14] From Byron-Curtiss' *Reminiscences*.

FROM TAVERN

The bishop very much disliked communion wafers, which he described as "a very thin, brittle sheet… dissolving of itself the moment it is placed on the tongue into a tasteless liquid, and passing down from the mouth by the aesophagus not as a solid substance but as a liquid, though scarcely known to any sense, [which] is not, to me, bread." The services of the church were to be carried out with "actual bread," commanded the prelate.

And while the right reverend bishop admitted that mixing some water with the wine was "without objection," if it was done in the sacristy, he stated that commingling the water and wine "as a visible part of the administration is, to me, inadmissible, being a form of individualism without the least recognized authority…" "To do it conspicuously with something like an ostentation of movement and cruet, indicates a certain disposition to self-will which need not be characterized." In 1901 such a ceremonial commixture, with a visible blessing of the water and a silent prayer by the priest, was considered very "advanced" and was in truth an imitation of Roman Catholic practice.

There were however no reasons to think that the rector of St. Peter's was anything but a loyal Prayer Book churchman whose leanings were on the protestant side. In 1902 Dr. Brainard preached on the first Sunday of Lent at the evening service of the Central Presbyterian Church.

From 1896 to 1899 Dr. Brainard's health and the volume of duties necessitated frequent assistance at the services on Sundays. His chief helper in this regard was often a Dr. Murray. In 1900 Dr. Brainard obtained the vestry's agreement to hire an assistant, assuring them that the young man of his choice, Mr. Leonard J. Christler, "seemed to possess many elements of promising usefulness." The rector apparently paid the assistant from his own pocket as there is no mention in the record of any payments to the younger man other than to reimburse him for some expenses and outlays on behalf of the church. [When Brainard later gave up any attempts to take services he told the vestry to use his salary to pay anyone they would employ.[15]]

When Bishop Huntington died in 1904 the published notice of sorrow was signed by "the rector, rector-coadjutor, wardens and vestry ..." That second title, 'rector-coadjutor,' applied to Mr. Christler, was utterly non-canonical and contained a very problematic note for the future. It was obviously an imitation of developments in the diocese, where the Rev. Charles Olmstead had, in accordance with canon law, been elected to succeed the venerable but still living Bishop Huntington. In 1902 Olmstead became the first priest to be elected as "bishop co-adjutor" for the Diocese of Central New York. Since the expression "rector co-adjutor" seems to be entirely of Brainard's doing, it shows his unwary intention to make Leonard Christler his automatic successor, thus eliminating any other choice by the vestry. Meanwhile Mr. Christler was busily cultivating the growing broader social base of the parish and developing a following among the local tradesmen and working class. A joiner, the popular young curate enjoyed membership in fire departments and several fraternal lodges. Twice he was asked to make a December 6th memorial oration at the Elks convention in Oneida.

In 1904, as there were no repairs to the church, Dr. Brainard was paid an additional $358.79, the interest from the Hulbert fund. A new water motor for the organ cost $135 which was contributed by some unnamed donor.

---

[15] John Brainard, who often lent the parish money and made contracts on his own, had private income.

From Tavern

In April 1905 the vestry declined to support a request to pave Genesee Street, on the grounds that many members of the parish lived on the street and opposed the project. Evidently the occupants of the finer homes to the west of the church had no desire to see their taxes raised. On August 10, 1905, Cornelia Fatzinger Brainard died at the age of 72. Dr. Brainard was too overcome to function. Leonard Christler officiated at the services at St. Peter's and accompanied the body to the cemetery in Waterloo where she was buried with her first husband, manufacturer Levi Fatzinger. The old rector ceased to make entries in his journal, and his health declined rapidly.

By 1906 the vested choir had been accepted. Sixteen new hymnals and sixteen new chant books were purchased for their use, and an architect was engaged to design a Robing Room and Toilet Arrangements in the chapel building.

When Dr. Brainard made it known in April 1906 that he wished to relinquish all responsibility for the services, petitions from church members and townspeople were presented to the vestry in May to confirm Leonard Christler as the new rector. The vestry declined to do so, finding the idea "inexpedient."

The depiction of the Tiffany Silver Pitcher below shows the 20 inch, one gallon gift on the occasion of the celebration of Dr. Brainard's twenty-five year anniversary at St. Peter's. The inscription on the pitcher reads:

To the
REVEREND JOHN BRAINARD, S.T.D.
from the Parishioners of
ST. PETER'S CHURCH, AUBURN, N.Y.,
in token of their grateful appreciation of
His Pastoral Care
During Twenty-five Years.
ALL SAINTS' DAY.
1863-1888.

Dr. John Brainard

Chapter 10

How John Brainard became Auburn

Any attempt at an evaluation of John Brainard necessarily derives in large part from the information provided by his journals. In them we learn that he took great satisfaction in the huge numbers of people he had baptized, married, presented for confirmation, and buried over his long ministry. From the very first his goal was to minister for a long time. In an age of progress his joy and medium of operation was the pursuit of growth. He chose for a field of continuous service a community which he judged to be an area of great growth potential and which was offered to him as such.[1] Over and over he renewed his call to Auburn because it was a field for success. When he took stock of his own ministry he placed the emphasis on numbers and continuity of service. Possibly he knew himself to be no great theologian. His sermons fit well with his advocacy of responsible citizenship and joyful participation in the burgeoning republic. Although he knew loss and deprivation, there is in his record no morbid dwelling on the tragic dimension of life. His pride in such a long ministry was to have ministered the offices of the church to generation after generation. By the end of the century only a handful of parishioners were left who had been present in 1863.

We know from his speeches that he had a good sense of humour and that he was renowned as a speaker on public occasions, at

---

[1] On his 36th anniversary in November of 1899 he said that he came to Auburn originally "for the apparent opportunities of greatly increased and successful work."

commemorations, and after dinner.² When he gave his benediction, or bestowed his approval, after those many decades of ministry, the blessing he offered embodied in clerical form the accolade of the community, as well as the approval of an institution that was as old and as successfully increased as Auburn itself.

He was a friend and peer of bishops. A brief period with Bishop DeLancey preceded his service under Bishop Coxe, his former rector in Baltimore. After the formation of the Diocese of Central New York he was a fixture on the Standing Committee of the diocese, the council of advice for Bishop Huntington. He served as a member from the inception of the diocese in 1868, was elected secretary of the Standing Committee in 1878 and made its president in 1886. On the occasions when the diocesan convention met in Auburn his witty invitations, convenient special arrangements for the railroad connections, and thoughtful hospitality, made the gatherings enjoyable for all who attended.

The primary impression to be gained is that of a very affable man, congenial with the successful, pleased with surviving in dignity and honor, very predictable and reliable, possessed of a great store of boardroom humour, who fit entirely into the comfortable life of his parishioners, and occupied a social position in the parish equivalent to that of its most prominent members. His struggles, few as they were, were to press his conservative, not always very imaginative, peers to finish in style the work they had been stimulated to undertake. He was completely acculturated to Auburn. Though twice mentioned as

---

² In 1904 the newspaper carried an account of a Country Club dinner for comic opera star Raymond Hitchcock which described Dr. Brainard as "once, sans surplice, there's not a better equipped storyteller in the universe." Hitchcock was a former chorister at St. Peter's.

bishop,³ he would not have left the pastoral equality he enjoyed with the prominent and the superiority he knew with the lesser orders.⁴ After the first few decades John Brainard could not have left Auburn because he <u>was</u> Auburn, from head to toe. In a city gradually gaining in polish, a community with which he also had grown, he wore his Connecticut origin as a badge of superiority. He had come westward from Hartford, a seat of established respectability in the east, to aid and to improve.

He was a realist about the chief source of the financial and professional support which he received from the parishioners. Though he said at times that he wanted to see an "endowment fund, with a view to making the church a free church in the future," he knew that such a plan would not succeed in his time. His private means gave him semi-independence and enhanced his status.

One view into his nature is provided in the reminiscences of the socialist cleric Arthur Byron-Curtiss, who when a young priest, often visited Dr. Brainard in the last years.

> St. Peter's church, Auburn, is an old parish. Rev. John Brainard was rector for something like forty years, as I recall. He was one of the Doctor's of Divinity of the diocese who never impressed me as a scholar. Somehow, he and I became particularly close friends. That friendship

---

[3] Once, among many other clergymen, for Indiana. In 1887, as a "compromise candidate" for Delaware. It was said then that Bishops Coxe and John Williams promoted his cause, and it was alleged that Seward "often said he would one day be a bishop."

[4] According to socialist Arthur Byron-Curtiss, Bishop Charles T. Olmstead's standard accolade for the people of any parish was that they were "eminently respectable."

may have evolved because both of us masticated tobacco at times and enjoyed 'telling stories.' He would scribble a note 'Come, make me a visit' or something like, enclose a couple of dollars in currency and mail it to me at Rome. If I had the time free, I'd go to Auburn and spend a couple of days.[5] It meant sitting up until one or two o'clock in the morning, smoking and telling stories. Always a few liquid night-caps ere retiring. He was one of the best reconoitre's [raconteurs] I ever encountered.

Dr. Brainard told me of all his troubles, squabbles and – triumphs he had with his vestry, in building the present fine church. The rose window in the west end, if one will note it, has the traceries of actual stone, instead of the wooden framework as in most churches. He told me he had an 'awful fight' with his vestry to carry that point; that it cost, as I recall, a thousand dollars more than if the traceries were of wooden frame. I recall the sum would have built a neat wooden chapel for some rural station. The West front does look very imposing from the street. But alas, here again the thrifty commercial way prevailed, even here. The clere story rests on wooden columns and the sides exposed to the weather are covered with a slate tile. St. Paul's, Syracuse, is the only church in the diocese I can recall, having an 'honest-to-God' clere story of masonry.

---

[5] Byron-Curtiss was a native of Waterloo, and enjoyed a chance to visit the area.

Dr. Brainard made much of the fact Bishop Hobart died in the rectory of St. Peter's, and in the old church, 'DeLancey rose from his knees, a Bishop.' This original church is now used as the chapel; stands just west of the present church, and a little back. As I recall, this building was taken down, stone by stone, and rebuilt in its present position, to admit of erecting the new church in a seemly location on the plot.

The last time I visited Dr. Brainard was the day Bishop Huntington was buried at Hadley, Mass.[6] The P M of the day the Bishop passed on, Ariah Huntington had wired me at Rome: 'Father passed on peacefully today.' On receipt of the telegram in Rome, I had caused the bell of our old mission church I was in charge, to be tolled the proper number of strokes to correspond to the Bishop's age. I got the telegram in early evening, and the tolling of the bell, as the twilight deepened, made a great and solemn impression among all the people in that part of Rome. As we were sitting in Dr. Brainard's study and thinking and speaking of the great man the Diocese had lost, I mentioned how I had had the bell tolled at old St. Joseph's. The good, active old man jumped up and almost taking me by the collar, said, 'come on,' and we hustled to the tower of St. Peter's and began tolling the heaviest bell in the set of chimes. It took us a long time to make the eighty two solemn strokes. But he masticated the weed and I burned it, while one would pull the striking lever and the other keep tally on a slip of paper.

---

[6] July 15, 1904.

> I know little about St. John's, Auburn, save that there was never any love lost between its rector and the rector of St. Peter's."[7]

John Brainard was a fixture at dinners and celebrations of a civic nature. A sample of his style can explain why.

In 1901 Mr. Benjamin B. Snow retired after laboring 31 years as the head of the Auburn School System. The rector of St. Peter's was one of a large number of speakers that evening, and his remarks were taken down. They provide an example of the humour and the brevity for which he had become loved in the city. The short speech is also revealing about the circles in which the old rector moved.

> Mr. President and Ladies and Gentlemen: We had a hail storm last Saturday and tonight we have a Snow-storm, a perfect outburst of love, affection, respect and appreciation for our dear friend and neighbor, Mr. Secretary Snow. An European nobleman, unfamiliar with American customs once asked another, 'What is the usual mode of procedure in marrying an American heiress?' 'It is very simple,' was the answer. 'You tell the lady how much you love her, and her father how much you owe.'
>
> Now Mr. President, all Auburn loves Mr. Snow, and we owe him more than we can ever repay. Now I have never had but one thing against Mr. Snow. In his pathetic letter of resignation of his office, to the Board of Education, he

---

[7] "Reminiscences of the Diocese of Central New York 1888-1950," Arthur L. Byron-Curtiss, unpublished manuscript, May 1950.

made use of certain words touching the duty of a man to resign all office when he has reached the age of 70 years. That is a most unsound idea to advance or maintain, and I take issue with Mr. Snow. I do not think it my duty to resign the rectorship of St. Peter's church till I resign my breath – and I am in no great hurry to do that. Mr. Snow did not desire to drop out because he had any fears of the future, because he is too much of a Universalist for that, and my wish to stay in does not come from any fears of the future, since my faith in God's loving fatherhood and trust in the infinite merits of His dear Son are so strong that I cannot but believe that He who has taken such good care of me hitherto will not let me drop out of His loving regard. To be just as good as I possibly can to such loving friends is the sum and substance of my religion: and I do not believe Mr. Snow's religion differs greatly from that.

I used to think Mr. Snow was destined to be a millionaire, another Carnegie or J. Pierrepont Morgan. I once saw, several years ago, an immense pile of small grindstones down Washington street. I asked a mutual friend what these things were. He replied, 'They are part of a great business, the manufacture of grinders for mowing machine knives, that will make some Auburn people as rich as Croesus,' and mentioned Mr. Snow's name among the favored group. He said it was sure to make millions, that every farmer on earth would have one. He also added that it was awful hard work to get any of the stock but that he knew where there was some of it to be got as a great favor, and perhaps I might be accounted worthy to come in. 'No thank you,' I said, 'Mr. Snow and the others are such worthy men, I will not attempt to rob them of their millions.' What I refrained from lodging safely here, I placed in the Tuttle works and the Clapp Wagon works, to illustrate, I suppose, 'that a fool and his money is soon parted.' I think that some of those grindstones can even now be seen in the lot near the Wringer company. 'The grinders have not ceased because they are few,' but because they were never put in motion. How fortunate, how very fortunate for Mr. Snow. If he had made his millions it might be thought that we were loving him for his great wealth, whereas we are loving him for himself.

I read the other day of a man called out from some banquet on important business and, having with him a valuable silk umbrella which he did not wish to lose during his absence, wrote on a card which he pinned to the umbrella as follows: 'This umbrella belongs to a man who weighs 240 pounds, of cruel and vindictive spirit, who thinks nothing of taking a man's heart out of him upon the slightest provocation.' He returned to find in place of his umbrella this card: 'Your umbrella was taken away by a small man of delicate and consumptive tendency, who weighs but 110 pounds; but he can walk 15 miles an hour and will never come back.'

Now, Mr. Snow, as we are willing to testify, has never been an umbrella to keep his auditors dry. But he has been a shelter and a protector to our children during all these years, while they were learning how to be useful and good, during the storms of life, by reason of his wise management of our public schools. And it is a pain and grief to us to reflect that when this sheltering umbrella is withdrawn it is not likely to come back. May God grant to you, my dear friend, every happiness in this life and a blessed hereafter in the Kingdom of our Father."

When the rector died on November 25, 1909, at the age of seventy-nine, the Auburn *Daily Advertiser* carried the obituary it had ready.

> Rev. John Brainard, D.D., rector of St. Peter's Episcopal Church, since November 1, 1863, died at the rectory just at the stroke of 6 o'clock, last night. It was the end of a life of great good and noble deeds, the termination of a pastorship of 46 years in one church and a lifework in the advancement of Christ's teachings. No man in Auburn ever had more friends and stauncher ones than the venerable rector of the St. Peter's church and his death is felt by hundreds as a personal loss. Ministering to families stricken with sorrow and trouble through nearly half a century in the city of Auburn, with them at the times of joy and happiness, Dr. Brainard was so closely associated with hundreds of people of the city that he became their personal friend, and to them the loss that is sustained in his death is a great one.
>
> Failing in health for three years, Dr. Brainard still maintained his position as rector of the church and it was not until a sudden change for the worse, considered at the time as only a temporary setback, came last week ago that it was seen that the time of the venerable pastor's long life was coming to an end.

After a review of John Brainard's life and work, the article continued: "He often referred to the many weddings at which he had officiated, and also to the hundreds of funerals at which he had conducted the services. In this way as well as in many others he extended his friendship, and the scope of his influence."

At the close of the obituary special notice was taken of his friendship with Auburn's National Guard and his close relationship with the St. George's Society and the annual pilgrimages which each body made to St. Peter's church. "The Cayuga Asylum for Destitute Children was another institution that knew him well and the custom of Christmas dinner was one that he established. He was closely connected with the Seymour library for many years and in other departments of the city life his influence made itself felt."

The Syracuse *Post Standard* carried this notice:

> Dr. John Brainard of St. Peter's church in Auburn, the learned, the witty, the genial and the beloved, is here no more. He was known throughout the length and breadth of the Episcopal diocese in this country, but in the diocese of Central New York he was a father to so many of the elder ones that the church in this part of the world was in fact his family.
>
> And not alone his church, but the city of Auburn, where he has ministered for forty-six years, looks back with gratitude upon Dr. Brainard's life and the cheery and manly religion it stood for."

The Auburn *Citizen* carried a full account of his funeral. The church was overflowing one hour before the three o'clock service on November 27. The bells tolled from the tower as professional pallbearers carried the casket from the rectory to the church, where it was covered with a purple pall, "almost concealed in violets and smilax." The family consisted of John Morgan Brainard and his wife Jennie, and Cornelia Fatzinger Brainard's daughter Mary and her husband Henry D. Noble. Twenty clergymen followed the vested choir of men and boys as the casket was borne into the chancel. Various clergy shared the service, conducted by the new rector, Mr. Houser. Bishop Olmstead pronounced the benediction. "At the conclusion, Rev. Norton T. Houser returned to the church and recited verses from the Scripture that had been particular favorites of the deceased. The members of the congregation passed the casket and viewed the remains, going out by the side doors of the church." The remains were to lie in state with a guard of honor until the New York Central evening train for Hartford, Connecticut. "The church will be open until train time for those who desire to view the body. The casket will be accompanied by Mr. and Mrs. John M. Brainard and Sexton Henry Whipps."

The vestry of St. Peter's had ready a tribute to the departed rector, which was printed after the *Citizen's* account of the funeral. The composition paid tribute to Brainard's strengths.

> During this unusually long period of service he has guided the business affairs of this church with great prudence and ability… While he was ever diligent in his labors for the temporal welfare of his charge, he was not less devoted to its spiritual life.

For nearly two generations he has guided and led his people along the paths prescribed by the church, and by his personal life perhaps as much as by his sermons has taught them the truths for which the church holds its high commission.

During all these years he has been a welcome visitor to our homes. He has rejoiced with us in our prosperity, has comforted us in sickness and has consoled us in the hour of bereavement...Such services of love and sympathy can never be forgotten....

His was a broad view. Not yielding any of the essentials of the faith and doctrine of our church, he was genuine in his appreciation of the work being done by other churches. 'In essentials conformity: in non-essentials unity,' expresses his spirit.

This mental attitude made it possible for him to establish and maintain lasting friendships with clergy of other denominations in this city and to cooperate with them in good works.

He has thus helped materially to lay the necessary foundation for that real unity among Christian churches which is the hope of so many leaders of religious thought today....

Thus at the end of the first century of St. Peter's existence, the denominational discord which had brought it into being found resolution in the personable character of its departed leader. While it is hard not to detect the hand of the Rev. Mr. Houser in this politically correct encomium to church unity, the reality was that John Brainard had lived on well beyond the period of competition into an era of pleasant coexistence, a time of "cheery and manly religion."

APPENDIX A:

THE DEATH OF BISHOP HOBART

by Cynthia McFarland

Making his visitation to confirm and officiate in upstate New York, Bishop John Henry Hobart arrived in Auburn on the first of September, 1830. Not very tall and wearing thick glasses, the energetic fifty-five year-old was the third bishop of New York and the first to make regular trips to the sparsely settled areas of his diocese. The bishop had achieved an enormous amount in his career. Writing and publishing to defend the significance of the apostolic succession which the Episcopal Church possessed in its bishops, he had founded a college in Geneva and the General Theological Seminary in New York.

Tireless pastor to the clergy, his travels over New York state were in addition to his duties as rector of Trinity Church, Wall Street. In his lifetime the number of the clergy of the diocese grew from 26 to 133, the parishes amounted to 126, and he confirmed about 20,000 people.

This lovable, indefatigable, hard-working bishop went nonstop from his entry into the ministry until his death in 1830. The surprise was that he lasted as long as he did.

At midnight September 7, 1830, a young clergyman rode the stage through Auburn on his way to Binghamton. Passing the rectory of St. Peter's Church, he was puzzled to see a light so late. He rapped for the stage to stop, and alighted. He soon learned from the rector, John

Rudd, that Bishop Hobart was ill. The Rev. Francis H. Cuming remained at the rectory to assist in any way he could.

Hobart's illness wasn't surprising. He had been troubled for years with what was probably a stomach ulcer, but with rest and medicine he had always rebounded. On this visit to Auburn, thought troubled with a slight cold, he had preached and confirmed at St. Peter's on September 2, and seemed fine that day. Yet by the evening of the 7th he was visibly worse. On the morning of the 8th he was convinced by John Rudd and Dr. Morgan, a local physician, to cancel his visit to a parish near Syracuse. The bishop realized that he was not well enough to finish the last two weeks of his grueling travels and decided to return to New York. He dictated a letter to his son, Dr. William H. Hobart, asking him to come to Auburn to accompany him home.

Hobart observed to Rudd that this was the third serious attack he had suffered and that such a one no doubt would be his end. He added, "Perhaps this may be the one; if so God's will be done. Pray for me that I may not only say this, but feel it; feel it as a sinner; for, bear me witness, I have no merit of my own."

Soon the ominous nature of the bishop's attack became clear. He requested to hear portions of Lancelot Andrewes' seventeenth century litany, in which he joined. Yet amid his pain, Hobart found opportunity to offer advice to Cuming: "Be sure that in all your preaching, the doctrines of the Cross be introduced: no preaching is good for anything without these."

Francis Cuming recorded: "Once having called upon me to use a short prayer, (his pains were so severe he could not give his mind to them unless they were short,) and when I had invoked our Heavenly Father to continue to be gracious to his suffering servant; and that whereas he had studied to approve himself to God upon earth, he might be permitted to stand approved by his Master in heaven, he interrupted me by saying, 'Amen: O yes, God grant it, but with all humility I ask it.'"

Bishop Hobart was in great pain all this time, which he compared with having burning lava filling his bowels. "This pain is dreadfully, inconceivably distressing; it is agony, agony. Yet what is it compared with that my Saviour endured? I will not complain. God's will be done."

On Friday, September 10th, just before sunset and as the last rays of the sun were playing upon the wall not far from the bed, the bishop said, "Open the shutters, that I may see more of the light; Oh how pleasant it is: how cheering is the sun – but there is a Sun of Righteousness, in whose light we shall see light."

At 9 p.m. that Friday, William Hobart arrived. Knowing full well that he was dying, the bishop assured his son that Dr. Morgan had been attentive and kind. "On receiving the slightest refreshment or relief," John Rudd later commented, "his first expression was 'God be praised,' and then he would tenderly and repeatedly thank the immediate agent."

Francis Cuming remembered that, "there were times when he was peculiarly oppressed. The promises of the Gospel, however, would revive him. At one of those times he said to me with the most remarkable emphasis, 'Comfort me.' The reply was 'Bishop, it is written, the blood of Christ cleanseth from all sin.' – 'So it is, so it is,' he added; 'God be praised for that; God be praised for all his mercies; God be merciful to me a sinner!' – 'You must all,' he said, 'commend me in your prayers to God's mercy. You are attending to my body – forget not that I have a soul to be saved. Pray for my soul.'"

On Saturday the physicians recommended that Hobart be told that he was near death. John Rudd quietly informed the bishop that if he had anything to do or say, there should be no delay, and asked his wish as to the Lord's Supper. "Oh yes," he said, "the sacrament; the sacrament; that is the last thing; that is all; let me have it." Firmly and with composure he uttered the words, "Well, God's will be done."

Dr. Rudd began the service. When he came, in the confession, to the words "by thought, word, and deed" the bishop stopped him and said, "You know the Church expects us to pause over those words; pause now, repeating one of the words at a time till I request you to go on." This was done, and the pauses in each case were so long that a fear passed over the minds of his hearers that he had lost recollection or fallen asleep. This proved not to be so; he repeated each word, and after the third pause added: "Proceed, I will interrupt you no more,"

Saturday afternoon Bishop Hobart dictated to Francis Cuming his last will and testament and gave him messages to deliver. Cuming asked for permission to kiss him farewell. And the bishop said, "I die at peace with all men, for I am sure I forgive all."

John Rudd sat with the dying bishop till well after midnight, into Sunday morning. "For about four hours before he expired he was nearly if not quite insensible to what was passing around him. He sank into the arms of death without a struggle, and his face soon assumed that engaging expression which in life so often delighted those who loved him."

On Sunday morning the body was placed in a coffin in the drawing room of the rectory. After inviting into the room those gathered outside the door, John Rudd made a few remarks and officiated at the service in the *Clergyman's Companion,* a manual which Hobart had compiled and edited.

At 3 p.m., when the coffin was placed on the hearse waiting before the rectory, the bell of St. Peter's was tolled until the procession reached the edge of the village. Several carriages proceeded with the body to Weedsport, eight miles away, where a canal boat was in readiness. Francis Cuming stayed with the remains of the beloved bishop throughout the trip down the canal and the Hudson.

The funeral took place in New York on September 16. The procession gathered at the rectory on Varick Street and walked at sunset to Trinity Church, Wall Street. The mourners included Governor Enos T. Throop and the Mayor of New York. The clergy of the diocese were joined by representatives of every denomination and of every society of which Hobart had been a part. The mile-long procession was estimated at nearly 3,000 persons, of which only a few hundred could fit into the church. At the conclusion of a service which lasted till after 9 p.m. the body of the sainted successor to the apostles was buried under the chancel of Trinity Church.

Leonard J. Christler

APPENDIX B:

THE REJECTED SUCCESSOR'S SENSATIONAL END

As the end of the nineteenth century approached John Brainard, Rector of St. Peter's Church, was nearing seventy. His accomplishment in Auburn was monumental, a parish with few financial problems, a magnificent cathedral and chapel, and many, many, of the fine families of Auburn in his congregation. His second wife, Cornelia, one year his senior, the widow of Waterloo manufacturer Levi Fatzinger, kept his household running in the old Federal period rectory next to the church. She had raised his son John Morgan as if he were her own, and managed his homelife as well as his late mother-in-law Mrs. Judson had done in her time.

Few pastors in the Episcopal Church had heaped upon them the memorials and distinctions that John Brainard received in the long years since he came to Auburn with his pregnant wife Marie Antonette and her widowed mother in 1863. From the first day it had been an exhilarating experience. On the train from Syracuse he had been accompanied by parishioner William H. Seward, the Secretary of State, traveling home from Washington to Auburn to visit his sick son. Met at the station by General John Chedell and a large crowd of leading citizens, the little family was conveyed grandly to their new home in the memorable rectory on Genesee Street, "Hobart House," as Brainard would later dub it. Brainard was a man to keep prominent track of his anniversaries, and he reveled in their accumulation. His Tenth Anniversary as Rector, would lead on to his glorious Twenty-fifth Anniversary in 1888, with its memorial booklet and a grand solid silver

From Tavern

Tiffany vase. To mark the close of his thirty-sixth year in 1899, two white oak trees were planted in front of the church. He had known and buried and shared in the honors of two great statesmen, Seward and Governor Enos T. Throop. He had been nominated for bishop several times, and while never elected, he enjoyed the distinction. <u>His</u> forte lay in his vocation as beloved parish pastor. He was President of the Standing Committee of the diocese and trusted counselor to his bishop. And he was a Morgan from Connecticut.

But advancing age and the increasing burdens of parish work made Brainard long for assistance, clerical assistance. The time when he had prided himself on the number of services he could conduct on a Sunday was in the past. Those days when he had taken three church services on the Lord's day, plus a baptism and several funerals, with possibly an evening service at St. John's thrown in, all in great stride, seemed to the aging priest to be long gone by. His success was his undoing. The wealthy were content to have their weddings and funerals and baptisms on days during the week. They took the time out or off as they pleased. But the growing numbers of the middling and lesser sort who flocked to St. Peter's because of the services and programs Brainard had helped put in place, these factory and day workers could not afford to take a weekday for their religious practices. They wanted their funerals and the like on Sunday, their day of rest and unemployment. Every year that went by, the journey to a home for a baptism or a funeral, or to the burial grounds of Fort Hill or Soule or North Street, in the rain or snow, felt harder and harder. The oak tree planted in his honor in the churchyard in 1899 grew stronger with each year, but the oak of a man from Connecticut grew weaker.

He began to look about for an assistant, perhaps even someone to take over near the end. There was no retirement as such possible. Even bishops served until they dropped. Bishops DeLancey and Coxe had soldiered on until their final breath in Geneva or Clifton Springs, confirming and preaching even when too weak to stand, bishop to the end of life. Perhaps John Brainard could engage a rector co-adjutor, an assistant enticed with the right to succeed him in office?

One fine day in late July of 1900 there appeared in Auburn the Rev. Leonard J. Christler, rector of Calvary Church, Homer, and a native son of Waterloo.[1] As Chaplain of the Triumph Hose Company No. 1 of Homer, he was called upon to make the response to the address of welcome in the first day's proceedings of the annual Central New York Firemen's Convention. At the same time Dr. Brainard's journal reads, "July 20. Friday: Began morning service in chapel but was taken sick and fainted. July 22. 6th Sunday after Trinity, ill in bed."[2] The twenty-four-year-old visiting fireman/priest was conveniently called in to take the Hutchinson-Guion wedding in emergency, "in place of Dr. Brainard who was indisposed."[3] A month later it was announced that

---

[1] Born in 1876, Leonard Jacob Christler was the second son of Henry L. and Mary Jane (Riley) Christler of Waterloo. The firstborn, George Washington Christler, arrived in 1876. A sister, Jessie Ann, was born in 1878, another sister, Effie May, in 1881. His brother Charles, born in 1884, was confirmed at St. Peter's April 2,1901, Leonard's first year as assistant. [Brainard recorded Charles confirmation as Charles Willard, although his name appears to have been Charles William.] As a twelve year old Lay-reader at St. Paul's, Waterloo, Leonard decided to enter the ministry. Graduating at twenty-one from St. Andrew's Seminary in Syracuse, he was ordained deacon October 4, 1896 in Trinity Church, Syracuse. He was then appointed to Calvary Church, Homer, and priested January 11, 1899. He began officially in Auburn on October 15, 1900.

[2] Brainard Journal III, 59

[3] Newspaper Clipping in Journal, "Assistant Rector for St. Peter's."

FROM TAVERN

Christler had been called to act as assistant rector to Dr. Brainard. He began to help on August 12th, 1900.

As the years passed Brainard began to style the young assistant "Rector co-adjutor." Though there is no such title in common use, it certainly carried weight and seemed to secure Christler as the guaranteed 'legal' successor to the old rector. Gradually Christler was taking more and more of the 'occasional' services of baptisms, especially those that were in the home or in the hospital, or of adults. His sister Jessie kept house for him, in their various apartments at No. 16 or No. 4 James Street, where she often stood as witness for the weddings performed in their small parlor. It is not fair to say that Christler completely took over, but by 1905-1906 he was performing eight out of ten weddings, most of the baptisms, and in 1905, all of the funerals and interments. John Brainard was plainly and practically out of commission. When Brainard's wife Cornelia Kern Fatzinger died in 1905 it was Christler who read the burial office. And he also officiated at the 1905 funeral of 81-year-old David Wadsworth, father of David M. Wadsworth, Jr., and grandfather of a recent Wells graduate, Miss Anna Wadsworth. The Wadsworths, with a fine large home at 186 Genesee Street, were the proprietors of the Wadsworth Scythe Factory on Wadsworth Street.

In April of 1906, Brainard, weaker, scarcely capable of public appearance, having made no entries in his clerical journal since early 1905, announced to the vestry of St. Peter's that he could no longer serve, and that he wished to give up his salary and retire to his lonely rectory. Yet somehow at this extreme, he managed to disengage Leonard Christler from the rectorship of St. Peter's Church.

One principal source for understanding why this took place is the account given by the Rev. Arthur Byron-Curtiss in his "Reminiscences" written in 1950.⁴ He describes Leonard Christler in the following unflattering passage.

> A Rev. Christler...had prepared for orders at St. Andrew's Divinity School.⁵ He came from a poor family of the village [of Waterloo], and I guess his success in entering professional life, together with a lack of grace, made the dear fellow awfully pompous, conceited and aggressive. He was assistant to Rev. Dr. Brainard...for a while. Dr. B was getting old and somewhat feeble, and Christler just rode over the old rector.⁶

How the break was achieved can be inferred from Brainard's letter in the vestry minutes of April 19, 1906:

"Gentlemen, as you are already aware no doubt, the Rev. Leonard J. Christler, my assistant, has resigned, and that his resignation has been accepted, taking effect at the close of the service on Sunday last."

That Brainard had precipitated some crisis to force the young man out, without alienating him fully, is indicated by the subsequent assertion of Byron-Curtiss that the old rector found his dismissed rector co-adjutor a new position appropriate to Christler's talents:

---

⁴ *Reminiscences of the Diocese of Central New York, 1888-1950*, by The Rev. A. L. Byron-Curtiss, typescript dated May 1950, preserved in the Archives of the Diocese of Central New York.
⁵ The small diocesan seminary in Syracuse operated for about thirty years, producing 80 graduates.
⁶ Byron-Curtiss, 17.

In despair, Dr. Brainard appealed to the young man's old rector, Dr. Duff at Waterloo. Between them they got Christler to go to Montana to do missionary work under Bishop Brewer. Bishop Brewer had been rector of Trinity Church, Watertown, and Dr. Duff told the Bishop to call Christler 'Archdeacon' and he would knuckle down and hustle the work. It worked out as they planned, and Christler even called himself by the usual flashy label, of 'Bishop of all outdoors.'⁷

But before Mr. Christler could be fobbed off to Montana, his friends in Auburn put up a struggle. He had joined a variety of fraternal organizations, the Masons, the Elks, and the Firemen. He was in demand as a speaker for these and had circulated widely in Central New York. Immediately that his *chute* became known, a petition campaign was drummed up in the newspaper⁸ and the vestry were troubled with petitions to keep him on, while Dr. Brainard was announcing the assistant's 'resignation.'

"Petitions presented on behalf of Mr. Christler were read and referred to the committee appointed to confer with Dr. Brainard," read the Vestry Minutes of April 19, 1906. They were dealt with at the meeting of May 2, 1906; "The special committee to whom the petitions on behalf of Rev. L. J. Christler was referred returned them to the Vestry for consideration... Resolved, that it is the sense of the Vestry that the

---

⁷ *Ibid.*
⁸ "Rev. Christler Must Stay" was the headline in the Auburn *Daily Advertiser,* April   20, 1906.

best interests of the Church made it inexpedient to comply with the requests of the petitioners."⁹

So the reason for excluding Christler from the rectorship was, that active as he might have been, he had worn out his welcome with Brainard, had overreached himself, and was not acceptable to the upperclass professionals and manufacturers who constituted the vestry of St. Peter's, and who now found themselves solely responsible for choosing the next rector. Byron-Curtiss makes clear that the assertive mill hand's son from Waterloo did not 'know his place.' A sure sign of the class conflict inherent in Christler's departure is the nature of his support. In addition to the fraternal organizations who "say that Mr. Christler can not and must not leave the city," a "delegation of laboring men visited Mr. Christler ... with a petition signed by two hundred laboring men." The laborers are stated to have offered him "generous financial support if he would make up his mind to remain among the citizens of Auburn." "All the parish societies" are represented as having petitioned the vestry on behalf of the young assistant, who visited the needy, ministered to the sick in the hospital, and played the Santa Claus to hundreds at Christmas time.¹⁰ The smell of opposition and competition, if not insurrection, was plainly in the air.

---

⁹ The vestry re-elected for St. Peter's Church on April 16, 1906, consisted of three factory owners, three wholesalers, two judges, a lawyer, and the superintendent of the Lehigh Valley Railroad. Five of them lived from numbers 186 to 250 on mansion row on the Genesee Street hill, and four lived within two blocks on fancy South Street.

¹⁰ *Daily Advertiser,* April 20, 1906.

From Tavern

But Leonard was wise enough to decline a public reception, offered "as a mark of the esteem and appreciation in which he is held by the men and women and children in all walks of life."[11] And the vestry held firm.

Thus Dr. Brainard was able to live out his years in the rectory until 1909, without having to contend with Leonard Christler's 'boorish' ambition. Instead the vestry found the old rector another 'assistant' in the person of the Rev. Norton T. Houser, rector of East Mauch Chunk, Pennsylvania. Mr. Houser arrived even before Mr. Christler was fully packed and proved himself diligent, professional, and sufficiently reserved to guard his circumstances. When Brainard finally passed away, Houser made it clear to the vestry that he did not feel entitled to become the rector automatically. The vestry elected him anyway.

Meanwhile Leonard Christler took to the West like a duck to water. Centering himself on Havre, Montana, the hub of the High-Line that runs east and west along the Milk River fifty miles or so south of Canada, his fraternal, social ways endeared him to many in the hundreds of square miles over which he ranged. Constantly calling himself 'the Bishop of All Outdoors,' he throve on the role of pioneer, working with the plainsmen, the miners, the homesteaders and railroaders, all of whom like himself he characterized as "wide between the eyes." There was room on the plains and valleys of Montana for his ambitious spirit. He was elected to a term in the state assembly. Over the years he saw the gradual building of a stone church in Havre, the granite for which was hauled free from Helena on J. J. Hill's Great Northern Railroad.[12] From the groundbreaking in 1908 until the first

---

[11] *Ibid*. This article in the *Advertiser* was accompanied by an extravagant three column, twelve inch high, photo of Christler in his robes.

[12] "Welch's Hi-Line Roofing Secures God's House," *The Havre Daily News*, August 6, 1999. Leonard Christler also served as a sponsored agent for

services in 1915 Christler pushed the construction along with a copy of the plans always in his pocket.[13]

But he did not neglect the folks back home. Annually the "Bishop of All Outdoors" returned to Central New York, where he cut a tall figure at over six feet, with a black coat that reached below the knee, his wealth of dark brown curls crowned by a sombrero that boasted of his Western home, and of his success. "He was quite a character. Not especially handsome, but you would know who he was if you saw him on the street," said a ninety-eight year old who remembered him from girlhood in Havre.[14]

In 1914 Leonard Christler returned to Auburn and wedded Anna Wadsworth, the scythe manufacturer's daughter. On October 7, 1914 they were married at her parent's home at 186 Genesee Street by his old rector from Waterloo, R. M. Duff. The actual Rector of Auburn that he might have been, Norton Houser, recorded the marriage in the register of St. Peter's Church, just a few steps away. There is no evidence that Houser was invited to the wedding. The witnesses were Thomas J. Walsh and Anna's sister, Mabel Wadsworth Pomeroy. Leonard was 37. Anna was 33.[15]

---

the Great Northern, lecturing in the East on the advantages of Montana life.
[13] Undated newspaper clipping from Charles Hurlburt's scrapbook, Christler File, Terwilliger Museum, Waterloo, NY.
[14] Louise Wigmore, *The Havre Daily News*, Jan. 3, 2001.
[15] Anna Wadsworth, born July 30, 1881, was the middle child of David M. Wadsworth, Jr. and May Crava Wadsworth. Her sister Mabel was born Feb. 1, 1878 and died in Buffalo May 13, 1940. A brother, David Wadsworth, was born August 6, 1887, and died in Auburn Dec. 14, 1923. David M. Wadsworth, Jr. died in Auburn August 16, 1922, having been a vestryman of St. Peter's continuously since 1901. His wife May

From Tavern

In a way they both were flawed for the marriage. He, shuffled off to the frontier, still considered pushy, marrying above himself said Byron-Curtiss, she, no beauty, always in black, probably not enamored of the rough West. "You know, Anna Christler, the wife, was tall, stately and dressed in black. She was not all that attractive. She was a sad looking character."[16] The Christlers remained childless through the eight years of marriage.

But they had friends, Judge and Margaret Carleton among them. When the Carletons broke up their marriage, the Rev. Mr. Christler did his best to counsel Margaret. She was a frequent visitor in the rectory and became familiar with its rooms and contents. As he comforted the estranged wife over a period of time it became evident that Mrs. Carleton had transferred her affections to the dashing minister and that perhaps the feeling was mutual. "We teenage girls followed his romance with Mrs. Carleton closely. We got a big kick out of that," remembered a Havre woman three-quarters of a century later.[17]

One week in October when Margaret Carleton returned from leading a tour on the "Chatauqua" circuit, she took up residence in a hotel room in Havre. Friends said she was "acting strangely." Anna Christler was under no illusions, Margaret was infatuated with her husband and wanted him for herself. Margaret kept hanging around their house, entering it when they were not home.

One Thursday evening in October of 1922, after special services at the church, Anna returned alone to the rectory next door, only to discover

---

died in Auburn July 22, 1935, *aet.* 77.
[16] Louise Wigmore, *The Havre Daily News*, Jan. 3, 2001.
[17] *Ibid.*

that someone was inside. Since Margaret Carleton had previously been observed wandering around and trying to gain entrance to the rectory, and since Leonard had spent part of the afternoon at Margaret's hotel room, attempting to soothe her, Anna called to a neighbor, Lawyer Hogue, to accompany her into her home. There they found an incoherent Margaret tearing up the rector's photograph. The lawyer and Anna persuaded Margaret to leave the house and Anna walked with her to the railroad station where they encountered Leonard putting the evening's guest preacher on the train to Butte. Margaret eventually went off, and about midnight the Christlers walked home to the rectory.

No sooner had they entered the house than Margaret Carleton appeared at the front door and walked in, telling Anna that she now had no place in Leonard's life. The couple attempted to reason with the woman but gained nothing. Leonard announced that he was going to bed and walked toward the bedroom. Anna turned to show Margaret the door. A shot rang out, Anna screamed, a second shot was heard. Leonard lay dead, crumpled in the doorway to the sleeping room, and Margaret, shot through the heart, was dead at his side, inside the bedroom or out. Anna summoned doctors and the police.

That is the account that Anna gave the inquest, at which she was the sole witness. The coroner's jury accepted it and ruled that Margaret Carleton had shot the minister dead and then turned the heavy revolver upon herself and with one more bullet through the heart had ended her own life.[18] Margaret Carleton's mother and the estranged husband, the judge, had another, uglier, version. Torn notes between Margaret and Leonard were discovered. But in a few days Anna was on her way back

---

[18] A .38 caliber revolver lay in Margaret's hand, but not the .22 derringer she was said to carry ordinarily.

to Auburn with Leonard's coffin, all expenses paid by the Masons of Havre, who sent two of their fellow craft to accompany her.

She wired the rector in Waterloo, the Rev. John Arthur, to arrange for a funeral in St. Paul's Church. She vowed that she would never leave her husband until his body rested in the grave. She kept her hand on the coffin for the entire sad journey. And she thought.

All the days and nights of the long train trip, she thought. What would become of her now? Her father was dead, her brother near death, her sister married and out of the home. Leonard had given her an identity, he had wooed the tall plain spinster and she had committed herself to him, had given up her identity in Auburn, had exchanged her place as the factory owner's daughter for one in a new town in a new state. Her sister had married a Pomeroy, that was a viable identity in Auburn. What would she be, without Leonard? One thing was certain, his honor and his memory must be upheld. Perhaps he had been incautious with Margaret Carleton, perhaps he had led her on until her fancy evolved into her fatal delusion. Surely it was not just a man who had done that, no it was a man of God, a servant of the Gospel. Leonard's fault, if it were one, had been to be too good, too open, too warm, too giving of himself. Acting in the spirit of the Gospel had brought him to his death. "He tried too hard to help people," she repeated to her sobbing heart, as the wheels of the railroad car clicked off the miles from brown, dusty Montana to green, watered, Auburn.

She would defend and preserve his memory. Her role now was that of the widow of a priest of the Lord. And she looked her best in black.

In Waterloo the incumbent rector, Mr. Arthur, mulled over the appropriate way to deal with the obsequies of this fallen brother. The papers had a field day with a juicy story, all the best ingredients of the journalistic stew; sex, religion, and violent death. From Syracuse the cowardly lion, Bishop Charles Fiske, wired that it would be inappropriate for Mr. Christler to have a church funeral. Mr. Arthur decided to overrule that on the scene, reasoning that Christler had not been under any sort of discipline. In consultation with Byron-Curtiss and the Rev. Henry Hubbard of Elmira, Christler's old classmate at St. Andrew's, it was determined to give him all the honors of his priestly orders.

And the Masons of Waterloo, learning of the manifest pride Mr. Christler had taken in Montana in his Masonic membership and of the generosity of the Blue Lodge of Havre, concluded to meet the funeral train at the station with a committee headed by the rector of Homer, the Rev. Mr. Pennington, a brother Mason, and to accord the Rev. Mr. Christler all the ceremonies of the Lodge. But before the train arrived and to their dismay, the good Masons of Waterloo discovered that Christler had not paid his dues for fifteen years and had been suspended from their fraternity. For the sake of the feelings of Mrs. Christler, their brothers in the West, and to cover their own embarrassment, they carried on with everything as if all were in order, "in the larger spirit of the Fraternity."[19]

The body of Leonard Jacob Christler, Priest, lay in state in St. Paul's Church, until four o'clock of the afternoon of Friday, November 3, 1922. Then, with the assistance of the Rev. Henry Hubbard of Elmira, and the Rev. Arthur Byron-Curtiss of Willard, the Burial Office was read by the Rev. John Arthur, Rector, and the interment followed in

---

[19] Details are from Byron-Curtiss.

Waterloo's Maple Grove Cemetery. The new widow took up residence with her widowed mother at 186 Genesee Street, Auburn.[20]

In the late nineteen-twenties, little David Hammond, serving the altar of St. Peter's at the eight o'clock Communion, was aware every Sunday of a lady, dressed in black, who sat in front of the pulpit, looking directly at the statues of the great preachers carved into its corners. Her eye could rest on St. Bernard, who preached a Crusade, or it might have preferred Savonarola, who brought about the 'bonfire of the vanities'. At any rate, when he asked his mother about the lady, he sensed a whiff of scandal when she whispered, "that's Mrs. Christler."[21]

"Hill Top Farm," the partially completed new home that Leonard Christler was building for himself and Anna, about a half a mile south of Havre, Montana, on the Beaver Creek road, was abandoned to the winds and fate. Never occupied, never lived in, it became a place for partying teenagers. One night it caught fire and burned completely. All that remained to remind of the virile minister was the tall rock chimney, with its two fireplaces.[22]

---

[20] In 1926 Anna Christler presented a pair of candlesticks to St. Peter's Church, in Leonard's memory, for use on the chapel altar. She later donated a large watercolor of Jesus and the Children, framed in polychromed wood, with a brass plate marked with his name and the year 1929. When Anna died in 1940 she was buried in Maple Grove Cemetery in Waterloo, next to Leonard and the Christlers and Rileys. A large marker, topped by a draped fallen cross, seems to have been provided by Anna. Leonard's headstone bears a cross, and hers, a slightly smaller one.

[21] Personal conversation with Dr. Hammond in 1995.

[22] *The Havre Daily News*, September 7, 2000. Alkali Springs Correspondent.

Courtesy of the Helmbrecht Studio
Havre, Montana

ROBERT CURTIS AYERS is a native of Roanoke/Salem, Virginia, and a graduate of Roanoke College and the Lutheran Theological Seminary in Philadelphia.

He served 22 years as the Episcopal Chaplain to Syracuse University, where he was awarded the doctorate in Philosophy in 1981.

He is Rector Emeritus of the Church of Saints Peter & John in Auburn, and he lives near Cazenovia, New York.

His most recent book is *Baroness of the Ripetta: Letters of Augusta von Eichthal to Franz Xaver Kraus.*

www.ingramcontent.com/pod-product-compliance
Lightning Source LLC
Chambersburg PA
CBHW030138170426
43199CB00008B/112